Styled for Living

A selection of residential projects from the pages of
Interior Design Magazine

Edited by
Sherman R. Emery, Editor,
Interior Design Magazine

Designed by
Alberto Paolo Gavasci,
Creative Director,
Interior Design Magazine

Foreword by
John Loring,
Design Director/Senior Vice President,
Tiffany & Co.

INTERIOR
DESIGN
BOOKS

Published by Interior Design Books
A Division of Whitney Communications Corporation
850 Third Ave., New York, NY 10022

Distributed by Van Nostrand Reinhold Company, Inc.
135 West 50th Street, New York, NY 10020

Copyright © 1983, by Sherman R. Emery
Library of Congress Catalog Card Number 83-50429
ISBN 0-943370-00-0

IDB Publications Director: *Virginia Evans*

IDB Publications Manager: *Chris Duffy*

Marketing and Rights: *Lusterman, Grybauskas Inc.*

Printed in Japan by Dai Nippon Printing Company through DNP (America), Inc.

Four-color separations: *Daiichi Seihan, Inc., Tokyo, New York*

Typography: *Elroy Typesetting Corp.;* Type: *Helvetica and Normande Condensed*

Mechanicals: *David Lance, Ilene Brown*
Balukas and Williams Design Group

Published by Interior Design Books, a Division of Whitney Communications Corporation, 850 Third Ave., New York, NY 10022

Distributed by Van Nostrand Reinhold Company, Inc., 135 West 50th Street, New York, NY 10020

16 15 14 13 12 11 10 9 8 7 6 5 4 3 2 1

Table of Contents

Introduction

This book is a compilation of residential projects published in the past few years by *Interor Design* Magazine, a professional publication edited for practicing interior designers.

What makes it different from other books on interiors?

Let's start by saying what it is not. It is not a "do-it-yourself" decorating book although it is quite possible that you will see in it ideas and innovative solutions to design problems that you can adapt to your own living needs.

Nor is it a coffee table book full of pretty pictures. To be sure, it is filled with handsome photography, but each photograph in each project was selected by our editors because it helped to explain the design process that took place when that interior was conceived.

What kind of book is it then? It is one in which every residence was executed by a professional interior designer. The information that accompanies each project explains in detail the design process, and although it describes the installation from the point of view of the interior designer, as related in interviews with our editors, the client's requirements and working relationship with the designer are always included.

Much has been written about interior designers and how they work, but this is the first book that, to our knowledge, illustrates through a variety of residential installations what the design process is all about.

Explaining the design process, however, does not necessarily answer all the questions which arise, especially from someone who may never have worked with an interior designer. Typical questions might be: "Will it cost more than I can afford?"; "Will the results look more like the designer than the people for whom he is designing?"; "If I have good taste why do I need a designer? What are the advantages of working with one?"

The cost will be determined by what you want to spend. Have a definite figure in mind when you begin. An experienced designer will be able to tell you if that figure is a realistic one to achieve what you want. Chances are it will not be enough. Good design is not necessarily expensive, but fine furnishings are. You may have to work in stages doing one room at a time. Some designers will work only on a prescribed minimum figure. Others work on a fee basis providing consultation service only and leaving the purchase of furnishings and other details to the client.

Interpreting personal needs and creating spaces to fit particular lifestyles are part of a designer's expertise. Most interior designers, however, do have a "style" or "look," and in many cases that style or look is the reason he is hired by a client. Also much of what you get will depend on the input you give the designer. The more information and details you give about your personal preferences, your likes and dislikes, the more of you will appear in the results.

The advantages of working with an interior designer are many. Today's designers are trained to do much more than put together a color scheme and select appropriate furnishings. They know scale and proportion; they can not only "decorate" a room but "shape" it to fit a client's individual needs; they can execute drawings for custom furnishings; they can specify architectural changes; and they know the multitude of sources for furnishings and materials, many of which are not available to the average consumer. They can also take on the many areas of responsibility which are perhaps best set forth in the official definition of an interior desgner recently adopted by the major design organizations including the American Society of Interior Designers:

"The professional interior designer is a person qualified by education, experience and examination who (1) identifies, researches and creatively solves problems pertaining to the function and quality of the interior environment; (2) performs services relative to interior spaces, including programming, design analysis, space planning and aesthetics, using specialized knowledge of interior construction, building codes, equipment, materials and furnishings; and (2) prepares all drawings and documents relative to the design of interior spaces in order to enhance and protect the health, safety and welfare of the public."

Everything that appears in this book was originally written by a member of *Interior Design*'s editorial staff. Since they are identified at the end of each article only by initials, we spell out their names in full below, for without them and their perceptive writing, this book would not have been possible.

E.C.: Edie Cohen • **M.G.:** Monica Geran • **L.W.G.:** Lois Wagner Green
F.K.: Ford Korper • **J.T.:** John Tucker

The old cliché that a picture is worth a thousand words is nowhere truer than in a design publication, and *Interior Design* is fortunate in being able to work with so many talented interior photographers. In addition to being identified with each installation shown, there is a directory of photographers at the end of the book.

The designers whose work is shown are listed in a separate directory. Space does not permit giving more information about them than an address and a telephone number. We feel, however, that the work a designer produces tells more about his talent than a dossier with education and personal details, and we hope that viewing the projects in this book will encourage you to consult one of them if you are considering having your home designed the professional way. The approach you can expect is well set forth in a statement made by Juan Montoya, the designer of the first project shown: "Whatever is done, it has to be right for the clients. That's the designer's job: not to embark on an ego trip, not to work by formula, but to accept the given challenge."

Sherman R Emery

5

Foreword

In February, 1983, Sherman Emery's editorial page of *Interior Design* was headlined "Glances at the Past/Hopes for the Future." What an appropriate sub-heading that would be for his *Styled for Living.* The tone and words of that editorial, so familiar to his broad and loyal public, restate his lifelong, impassioned, and highly successful crusade for *professionalism* in interior design as he welcomes a recent legislative act in Alabama prohibiting the use of the title "interior designer" by those who have not passed a state qualification examination. Further in his editorial comments, he expresses his also familiar hopes "to promote better design in America" and find additional means "to exhibit good design to the public."

These hopes have, of course always been Sherman Emery's business and, under his guidance, *Interior Design*'s business. He has been now some thirty years at *Interior Design,* years that have seen that fine review grow from the half-way point between the eight-page trade publication it started out as in 1932 to its present-day size and stature with a circulation of 50,000 that includes every enlightened professional in the business; thirty years that have seen American design evolve from the brave old eclectic Modernism of the 50s to the Post-Modernist architectural ornamentalism of the 80s; but, most important, thirty years that have seen attitudes change from the widely held view that "interior decorator," as designers were then called, was a suspect title to the near universal acceptance of interior design as a true profession, years that have seen, as Sherman Emery puts it, the separation of "the competent from the incompetent."

Who more than Sherman Emery can lay such claim to a position of influence throughout that long period of transition and progress, years through which he ". . . insightfully documented, intelligently applauded, and effectively nurtured . . ." quality and professionalism in the interior design industry as he presented in his review not just "jobs," not just things, but the talent and ideas that make for "living in style."

In the pages of *Interior Design* he, successfully again, fought against the tenacious fiction that the *soi-disant* "good taste" of amateurs armed with the slogan "I know what I like" and other such old chestnuts can deliver good design. He has taught us that "to know" what is desirable in design terms is the result of sound education and experience and that good design is not an evident result of simply harmonizing forms and patterns and colors through healthy intuitions. He has taught us that beyond those basics there is a feeling of place, a mood—yes, "style" itself—that is also and necessarily established by not only imagination but by such technically intricate sciences as acoustics and lighting and space planning—most surely all fields for informed professionals.

Styled for Living, an essay on that "Mercurial" (and therefore "Hermetic") quality without which there is no real competence in design, demonstrates what every designer, every purveyor of goods to the design industry, everyone interested in the quality of life must know:

Specific "styles" are definable and there for any and all to imitate at will, but Style itself is evanescent and inimitable. "Styles," whether "Victorian," "Edwardian," "Art Nouveau," "Art Deco," "International Modern," "Early American," "French Provincial," "Louis XV," "Charles X" or "German Knuttle," are only groupings—even if sometimes intricate groupings—of simple conventionalities that are fixed, repeatable and impersonal. A "style" is work finished. It may also be "stylish," but style itself is a far different thing. It is a work in progress, a flair fed by a vigorous and well-nourished imagination. To live with style is to run with a wave whose crests and currents resist the dangerously muddying undertow of those two great spoilers of design, sentimentality and pretention. Style runs naturally with the human bent towards order, proportion and internal harmony. Its only limits are the limits of the mind, the limits of imagination itself.

Through the purposefully varied sequences of outstanding interior designs from the recent past that make up *Styled for Living,* Sherman Emery does not give us a mere catalogue of the personal styles of a galaxy of today's most accomplished designers but a demonstration of style at work. *Styled for Living* is a focused and revealing image of the "design process," boldly underlining once more that design is a process whose function is to abstract—to "stylize," if you will—to "draw" from and on ideas in the shifting environment, to "draw" on its moods as it follows its cyclical course of eternal returns to the already-known before it moves on in the light of ever-expanding knowledge and re-evaluates, re-interprets, re-news.

Styled For Living: "Glances at the past, hopes for the future." Good news.

John Loring
East Haddam, Conn,
Sunday, May 1, 1983

Chapter 1

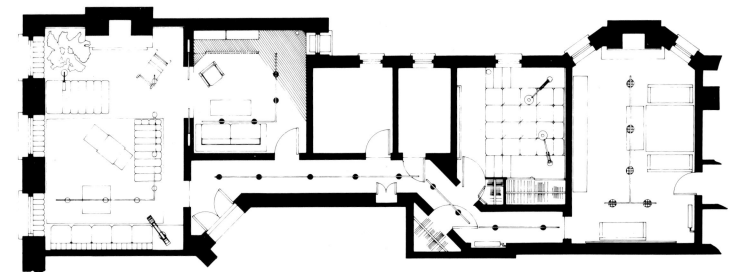

Upholding the Heritage

*Juan Montoya preserves
the late 19th century flavor of a
contemporary-in-feeling Manhattan residence*

They scraped and sanded the floors. They chipped the plaster from walls to expose bricks, stripped layers of paint from mouldings, uncovered and restored the fireplaces. They moved in some brought-along possessions: two fine bookcases to use in the living room, a round dining table, a few odd chairs, and a big brass bed. Then three long live-in years of loving labors later, they knew the place still didn't look right. Professional help was needed.

They, as might be guessed, are the clients, a young couple with careers in publishing and investments. The place is a cooperative floor-through apartment in an 1882 Greenwich Village (New York) townhouse. And the professional help they engaged came from Juan Montoya whose work was known to them through friends and through published articles in *Interior Design.*

Montoya saw the apartment and surveyed its credits and debits. On the positive side, he particularly liked the proportions of the rooms. He even took to the segmented corridor-bound layout, appreciating its uniqueness as a hallmark of New York's historical/architectural heritage. On the other hand, much of what he saw he found confusing: too much clutter, no sense of cohesion, harsh stone textures overpowering the richness of woods, furniture placed at odds with prevailing scale and dimensions.

Aside from visual distortions there were functional deficiencies. Closets were nonexistent, traffic flow was tortuous, and no plans had been made to take into account the couple's living habits. Quizzed by Montoya, they had indicated that they liked to entertain; that they enjoyed listening to music; and that they valued the views as seen from their sixth-floor windows. The designer analyzed their patterns of motions, too. What, he asked, do you do first upon entering the apartment? Where do you drop off parcels? Which routes do you follow when and why? From all these questions emerged

a series of guidelines influencing the eventual design scheme.

Aesthetically, the several rooms now are unified through repetitive use of white walls and industrial carpeting (only in the main living area and dining room are floors not fully covered). Serenity rules in the living room where the raw textures of exposed brick have disappeared under white-painted sheetrock leaving only one vertical surface, facing the fireplace wall, as found. Sofas provide islands for seating and conversation while preserving the sense of spaciousness. Cushioned ledges transform windows into lookout points freely accessible, Montoya points out, without anyone's tripping over the furniture. A large Bokara rug, from the small selection of belongings retained at the request of the owner-occupants, lends not only color and pattern interest but also softness underfoot in deference to the distaff resident who, under questioning, admitted that even as she enters the flat she kicks off her shoes. Also for her convenience, a small drop-shelf for parcels is at hand right next to the door.

Living room, its previously brick-exposed walls recovered with white-painted sheetrock, now appears larger and lighter. Three window ledges were cushioned to serve as vantage points for street watching, as extra seating, and hiding place for hi-fi speakers. Mirrors near restored fireplace reflect the single retained stone-textured wall and seem to extend the overhead track lighting. Bolstered loung and mobile table with pull-out panels were designed by Montoya; the Bokara rug and rocking chair were brought along from the clients' previous residence.

Photographer: Jaime Ardiles-Arce

Upholding the Heritage

In the study the relocated bookcases, elevated to showplace position, are reached from a step-up ledge covered with channel-patterned Pirelli rubber. Frequently doubling as seating, this walkway tops storage cabinets and drawers for music equipment and miscellany. Brass, repeating the material of bookcase fixtures, is used for the railing and door pulls. The bedroom has been filled with carpeted platforms holding the mattress and hiding storage. This horizontal arrangement counteracts the formerly off-putting impression of vertical imbalance created by the 10'-high ceiling above the 10 by 13' small space. For the 12 by 19' dining room, Montoya considered furniture in Mission or Shaker styling settling, after research, for the latter's less stark yet unfussy simplicity. His own interpretation (Shakers wouldn't have used cushions, he notes) of the style is applied to the banquette and benches framing the table, all massive-looking but easy to move. Off-centered, the furniture leaves ample free space and lets the warmth of the wood set the theme.

Since Montoya's work—perhaps unjustly—has come to be identified mainly with sleek all-contemporary design, one well might ask: Faced with existing restrictions, was he forced to compromise? Had it not been for the time and efforts spent on prior restoration, would he have removed the mouldings and trims? In short, if handed carte blanche, might the results have been quite different?

The first question Montoya counters with an unqualified "no," the others he considers irrelevant. "There never was any thought of what *could* have been," he notes, "only what *is* matters. And whatever is done, it has to be right for the clients." Concluding, "That's the designer's job: not to embark on an ego trip, not to work by formula, but to accept the given challenge."

Hardly the most original tenet, and easily shrugged off as so much rhetoric. But valid, it so happens, in the case of Montoya. One need only listen to any of his clients to know that his words and work sustain the promise. **M.G.**

Brass-trimmed bookcases, long in the owners' possession, assume focal position on the step-up walkway in the study/library/guest room. Surfaced with channel-scored rubber, the elevated ledge provides easy access to books and tops storage space for the music system. Brass is repeated for hand rail and hardware.

The 12 by 19' dining room appears even ▶ larger since the off-centered furniture, adapted by Montoya from Shaker styling, allows the warmth of oak wood to predominate. Niches aside mirror-topped fireplace were painted dark to read as shadows, floors were bleached and re-stained. The hanging quilt is from the clients' collection.

Horizontal platforms in bedroom optically reduce semblance of vertical preponderance caused by relation of 10'-high ceiling to small 10 by 13' space below. Storage space is provided by drawers under bed, carpet-covered wells on either side, and double closet, far right, created from furred-out wall niche. Windows throughout dispense with view-concealing treatments.

Three-Way Collaboration:
Client, Designer, Builder

A Lake Worth residence designed by Michael de Santis, ASID

Michael de Santis, ASID, receives credit not only for the interiors but also for the plan of the Palm Beach residence pictured on these pages. For he worked with builder Robert W. Gottfried from the planning stages onward.

Overlooking prestigious Lake Worth, the house is a two-story structure encompassing approximately 5500 square feet. The client couple's living quarters are completely contained on the first floor; servants' quarters comprise the second level. The plan was determined with the clients' participation. They did not request a large number of rooms—only a master suite, guest room and den to augment the "public" living room, dining room and den. They did, however, want individual areas to be amply sized, and that they are. The plan offers built-in flexibility since the clients are prominent members of the Palm Beach social set. Sliding doors between rooms allow the house to be opened up for large parties or closed off for smaller gatherings.

As for the decor, de Santis was granted virtual carte blanche in matters of both style and budget. The clients, to whom the designer attributes excellent and decisive taste, asked only that the finished product be "sophisticated and elegant, not apple green and white." De Santis met the directive through use of classic furniture forms, most of them custom designed; interesting detail work such as the lacquer and Lucite entry arch; and luxury connoting materials—velvet and satin upholstery fabrics, marble flooring and custom lacquer treatments. Particularly noteworthy is the master bedroom with its upholstered bed treatment and built-in electronic control system, completely operable from the bed.

Artwork and accessories, too, contribute to the required overall impression of elegance. The client already had an impressive collection, including the large Trova statue prominent in the living room. Other works were purchased as a collaborative effort between clients and designer.

Concluding, de Santis remarks that this was a problem free job, despite the tight time schedule alloted. "And," he adds, "everything had to be perfect the first time." Thus, furniture was designed and/or ordered as soon as plans were finalized. The entire project was completed—from planning to complete furnishings installation—in about eight months. **E.C.**

Opposite: View of the lanai or garden room, which overlooks a pool and Lake Worth. This informal room is separated from the living and dining areas by sliding doors (see plan).

Photographer: Jaime Ardiles-Arce

Two views of the living room. Custom-designed lacquer and Lucite arches lead to the entry foyer (opposite, right of photo) and dining room (above). The seating configuration was difficult to establish, de Santis says, because the room has no wall space; it is basically a pass-through. The white upholstery fabric is stitched velvet; the beige is satin. The large Trova sculpture had been in the client's collection.

Three-Way Collaboration

Continuing Commissions
Michael de Santis, ASID, designs
a cooperative apartment
for on-going clients in Manhattan's Galleria

Repeat commissions from satisfied clients are what every designer hopes for; he already knows their tastes and has won client confidence. This was the case, as it frequently is for Michael de Santis, ASID, with the owners of this cooperative apartment in Manhattan's prestigious Galleria building. Prior to this project, de Santis had designed the couple's Palm Beach residence (see preceding four pages); subsequently, he has completed their Southhampton, Long Island townhouse condominium. This on-going relationship, says de Santis, is particularly satisfying since the clients have sophisticated tastes that closely parallel the designer's own.

De Santis made only a few structural changes to the floor plan—basically an open living/dining space distinguished by what is termed a glassed-in winter garden overlooking 57th Street. The designer removed the doors that set off this area, thereby integrating it into the main space. He also created an enlarged master suite from what were originally two bedrooms; now each partner has his own bath and separate closet/dressing space.

Most of de Santis' work, then, centered on surface treatments, about which the clients expressed only a general request. They wanted the Manhattan apartment to look substantially different from the Palm Beach residence, which is pastel-toned, in keeping with its surroundings, and chic, but without the city-inspired drama associated with de Santis' work.

This page: View of the mirrored entry foyer where the strong blue and white color palette is established. The carpet's pattern was developed along with that of the upholstery fabric; the two are complementary. The painting, purchased by the clients from a Venetian gallery, is by Giorgio Zennaro. The double-head sculpture is by Jens Fleming Sorensen, and was purchased through the Crown Gallery in Copenhagen.

Opposite: Probably the two most striking elements in the apartment are this de Santis-designed stereo/television cabinet in stainless steel, and the wooden sculpture on top of it which has been authenticated as a 325 B.C. Egyptian sarcophagus mark.

Photographer: Jaime Ardiles-Arce

Views of the open living/dining space. The photo below shows the whole area and its reflection in the mirrored panels that flank the upholstered section of the end wall. The "winter garden" **(rear ground, left)** is integrated into the main area by seating that curves around to meet the back of the living room sofa **(see plan).** Columns were mirrored to disappear into the cityscape views, one of the apartment's chief assets. The sculpture on the desk behind the sectional seating is by Giorgio Zennaro.

Continuing Commissions

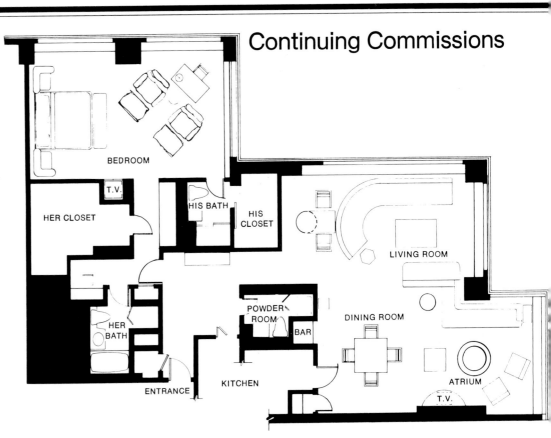

BEDROOM

T.V.

HER CLOSET

HIS BATH

HIS CLOSET

LIVING ROOM

HER BATH

POWDER ROOM

BAR

DINING ROOM

ATRIUM

T.V.

ENTRANCE

KITCHEN

Continuing Commissions

Granted *carte blanche* in his selections, the designer established a harmony throughout the space by using the same carpeting, vertical blinds and surface mounted overhead lighting. ("We couldn't get into the ceiling to do recessed lighting," says de Santis). He then built a strong background based on a navy blue and off-white palette, accented by mirrored columns and wall sections. Into this background he inserted slightly over-scaled furniture forms, the majority of them custom

What were formerly two bedrooms were restructured so that each partner could have a private closet/dressing area and bath off a single bedroom (see plan). The room, which also has a spacious sitting area and desk for the wife, is in tones of bone and pale lavender, the latter used for the ceiling color as well.

designs. As is his wont, de Santis worked with materials and finishes that connote luxury: stainless steel, lacquered parchment and faux ivory finishes; real ivory insets for detailing; handpainted silks and blue velour for upholstery covers. Probably the single most striking element is the custom designed stainless steel cabinet for television and stereo equipment. Its form is emphasized by its placement—framed by a midnight blue upholstered wall—and by the Egyptian wooden sculpture placed on top of it.

Although there is an intriguing collection of art shown, the apartment was not designed specifically as a display vehicle for it. In fact, de Santis explains, the clients purchased most of the works themselves after the apartment's completion. Could less than quality purchases have detracted from the designer's statement? Perhaps. But, de Santis, well acquainted with his clients, knew there would be art and knew that it would be good. **E.C.**

A Pavilion in the Trees

The Bellinger residence by Powell/Kleinschmidt
in St. Simon's Island

Background

Owners of the pictured residence are Mr. and Mrs. Kenneth Bellinger (whose daughter Gretchen is principal of the fabrics firm that bears her name). They have a year-round house in Connecticut filled with traditional furnishings and fine antiques. When they purchased property on St. Simon's Island, Georgia for their second dwelling, they engaged architects/designers Don Powell and Robert Kleinschmidt to design both the structure and its interiors. The architects were selected because they and Gretchen previously had worked together in the Chicago office of Skidmore, Owings & Merrill.

The designers on design:

"**W**e believed in something—that the space we were designing was universal." Thus Robert Kleinschmidt, speaking for himself and his partner, responded to this writer's initial query: If you knew the family, their background, and their strong penchant for things traditional, what made you think that they would accept something so different? Continuing, Kleinschmidt remarks: "We were building in 20th century ways. What we were doing was entirely appropriate for the client and his needs. The house had to be different from the house in Connecticut, or there would be no sense in coming to it."

To understand the design of the house, one must first recognize the strong attraction the physical site had for the client. The entire island is dense with a special variety of oak tree, and in fact, it was one such tree that swayed the client into purchase of this particular lot. "The oak trees set the atmosphere for the island," says Mr. Bellinger. "Otherwise, the island is flat—only ten feet above sea level." Knowing of their client's feeling for the site and of his passion for gardening, the de-

signers sought to make the house "a space enclosed by trees and gardens. It's designed as a pavilion in the trees."

The plan of the house, worked out primarily by Powell with close client collaboration, is based on a U-form. The central living room acts as the principal circulation route, providing a pass-through from the kitchen/dining ell to the sleeping wing. The house encompasses some 2200 square feet, but appears larger due to the walled-in courtyards that run the length of the east and west elevations (see plan). With full-height sliding glass doors opening onto these outside spaces, the courtyards are aptly described as open-to-the-sky rooms. Further, explains Kleinschmidt, they function to increase privacy and security, and solve the problem of undesirable views.

Once inside, the orientation is to the rear and sides of the house, which are glass window-walls. The front of the house is without apertures except for the carport which is integrated into the house, and the entrance door. "There are no windows because there is nothing at which to look," is Kleinschmidt's explanation.

$$\frac{1|2}{3}$$

Opposite are three views showing the entrance with its double doors (1), the courtyard and hallway along the kitchen/dining wing (2), and the front of the residence (3). In the hallway view, Kleinschmidt points out that the structural cross-shaped beams of painted carbon steel become sculptural elements. The custom cabinet (right of photograph) accommodates a temperature-controlled wine storage unit at its left end and a wardrobe for the front entrance at its right end. The perpendicular element (only partially visible in the rear) becomes the serving credenza for the dining room. The exterior view shows the massive oak tree responsible for the Bellingers' purchase of the property. It has been linked to the house by a foot-high wall that encircles the planting bed. The architects' concern for detailing extends to the carport; there are five skylights over the storage shed **(left)** to provide natural illumination.

Photographer: Bill Hedrich, Hedrich-Blessing

A Pavilion in the Trees

This page: A library, bedroom and bath are all part of the master suite that, along with a guest bedroom and bath, constitutes the private wing of the residence. In the library, the table/desk and shelving were custom designed. In the bedroom, detailing extends to the full-height louvered closet doors that had to be redone several times before meeting the architects' approval.

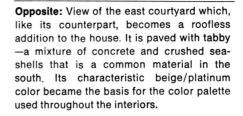

Opposite: View of the east courtyard which, like its counterpart, becomes a roofless addition to the house. It is paved with tabby —a mixture of concrete and crushed seashells that is a common material in the south. Its characteristic beige/platinum color became the basis for the color palette used throughout the interiors.

A Pavilion in the Trees

Once the structure was planned, Kleinschmidt set to work on the interiors. He was intent on proving to his client that "contemporary didn't necessarily mean stark. Mr. Bellinger appreciated quality things in a traditional way. If we were going to sell him, we had to somehow refer to traditional things." Thus, materials were selected for their qualities of warmth. Teak panels the dividing walls and custom cabinetry that become "massive sculptural forms in space." All hardware and metal are yellow-toned (brass or bronze) instead of silver finished. Materials were also selected for their appropriateness to the region—quarry tile and sisal carpet insets are flooring materials; upholstery fabrics are cotton or silk; much of the seating is of rattan. The pervasive beige palette was selected because it complemented an indigeneous building material called tabby—a mixture of crushed seashells and concrete used to pave the courtyards.

Without conscious effort, the designers provided an Oriental quality to the residence through simplicity, the quality of materials and attention to detailing. Design of the interiors was a paring down process. "We reduced elements to their functional minimum," says the designer. "Yet all elements are related so that subtracting one item would detract from the whole statement."

Both designer and client commented on the importance of lighting. Lamps were used only where needed for reading. Otherwise all illumination comes from recessed fixtures that are on rheostat controls. "Many of the walls are illuminated with wall washers to accentuate the architectural planes of the house," says Kleinschmidt. Exterior lighting is important too. Uplights, also on rheostat control, spotlight the large oak trees. When brightened against a dim house, they provide nighttime drama.

Client/designer interaction:

The designer describes his client as a perfectionist with definite opinions. "Determination is the key word in describing him. For this reason the house was a great challenge to us," he says.

Mr. Bellinger had his doubts about the house from the early design-on-paper and actual model stages right up to its completion. "It took at least two weeks to get used to it," he says. "Now I think it's terrific."

Early planning was filled with differences of opinion. The client originally perceived the plan as revolving around an atrium; the designers instead implemented the two lateral courtyards. For four months, designers and client argued over the roof design. He wanted a pitched roof; they wanted and finally got a flat one. Both, however, were sold on the concept of fitting the house to the landscape and the region. Both wanted the house to reflect the concepts of comfort and gracious living that was intrinsic to the Bellinger life.

The house is functional—practically maintenance-free —comfortable, and exquisitely detailed, says its owner. "All of the details are subtle and work together to produce an effect. You really have to be there over a period of time to appreciate them." Some of these details include: use of eight-foot frameless doors throughout; double front doors to provide a greater sense of entry; carefully placed lighting; and even unobtrusive baseboards (2½" instead of the usual 4-6").

Concluding, the client comments: "They accomplished their ends, but in the beginning we had our doubts. We went along with the plans because we had faith in the architects. The whole project was an act of faith."

The general contractor was R. B. Martin; the local architect was William P. Hooker.   **E.C.**

The client:
Kenneth Bellinger

The designers/architects:
Robert Kleinschmidt and Don Powell

Flexibility is the Keynote

*Udstad/Dandridge Design a Multipurpose
Apartment for a Fashion Illustrator*

The following dialogue is an edited version of a taped interview with the client and the interior designer describing the design and execution of a Manhattan cooperative apartment. George Dandridge was spokesman for the design team.

The client: *Charles J. Dillon,
a fashion illustrator who works in his apartment*

The interior designers: *Sid Udstad and George Dandridge
of Udstad/Dandridge Associates*

I had never worked with a designer before, but I decided that this time I wouldn't waste money and would have it done right. I went to Udstad/Dandridge because we were friends, but more than that I had seen examples of their work published and was impressed by them. I also felt that they wouldn't dictate to me and would interpret what I wanted.

I had one very specific need—studio space in which to work. I draw from live models so there had to be room for them to pose without interference of furniture. I also had to decide whether to use the living room as a bedroom and sleep on a sofa-bed or whether the studio should serve that purpose. We decided that a bed that goes into the wall would be more comfortable than a sofa-bed for everyday use and so the studio room serves a double duty.

I also liked the idea of keeping the studio distinctly separate from my living quarters. Since I work most of the day in the studio which is white and efficient looking, I agreed that contrasting dark brown walls would provide a more relaxed atmosphere in the other areas which are used mostly at night.

Another requirement I made was to be able to display my art collection which includes several fairly large canvases. I like the way they kept the walls free of furniture so that it doesn't interfere with the paintings, and I also like the built-in lighting which I can adjust if I decide to move paintings around.

When I approached Udstad/Dandridge to design the apartment, I naturally had a figure in mind that I wanted

In some ways, it was more difficult to work with Charles because we were friends. If things don't work out with the average client, all you've lost is a client; in this case, if things hadn't turned out well, we would have lost not only a client but a friend. Also some clients never really know what they want or what to expect, and when they see the results, they can be terribly disappointed. This was not a problem with Charles because our tastes are very similar, and being an illustrator he could more readily visualize what we proposed. For most clients, we provide renderings. In this case, most of our presentation was verbal rather than visual; we showed him floor, ceiling and lighting plans and a few elevations to explain the custom cabinetry.

OPPOSITE PAGE

To retain a feeling of height and disguise the awkward placement of beams in the living room, the designers mirrored the ceiling; adjustable ceiling spots, on dimmer controls, are focused on the art including a large landscape by Roger Nelson and a painting of nudes by Stephen Pace. The sofa was owned by the client but re-upholstered; the coffee table, lamps and console were also existing.

Photographer: Jaime Ardiles-Arce

Flexibility is the Keynote

to spend, but as we worked out plans together I realized that my original figure was wishful thinking, and in the end the budget was expanded by about one third. I was told, however, that I could cut corners in several places if I wanted to—we didn't have to have the mirrored ceiling in the living room, for example, nor a bathroom entirely of marble. They also suggested that I could wait for some of these things to be added later, but I decided to spend more and have better quality materials.

Although I'm pleased with everything in the apartment, the thing that really impressed me about their work is the superb way they coordinated everything. I purchased the apartment in early January and when I moved in on April 15th, everything was in place down to the last ashtray. □

Two things were given main consideration—providing a plan that would offer flexibility in the use of the space, and cleaning up some of the architectural background. The apartment is located in a wonderful old building, but like many similar buildings in New York, it has beams all over the place and other unattractive architectural details. We lowered the ceilings throughout to hide the beam breaks, but we didn't want to lose advantage of the height, so we recommended adding mirror to the ceiling in the living room and that creates reflective wells between the beams. Another major change was brought about by enclosing the old radiators with custom marble-top units; they not only conceal the radiators but also provide some extra storage space.

We also closed off a door that led from the kitchen to the bathroom giving more space in the bathroom and providing a solid wall in the kitchen so that we could create a dining area. And we eliminated arches between the rooms and made the partitions full height.

Although, as Charles has explained, the budget was increased as we went along because the original figure was not sufficient to achieve the results he wanted, we did advise him that cuts and substitutions could be made, and some suggested changes were dropped because of the extra cost, such as removing all the old baseboards and door frames. Actually, when the contract was awarded—three contractors bid on it—the budget set at that time was very closely adhered to and few changes were made. □

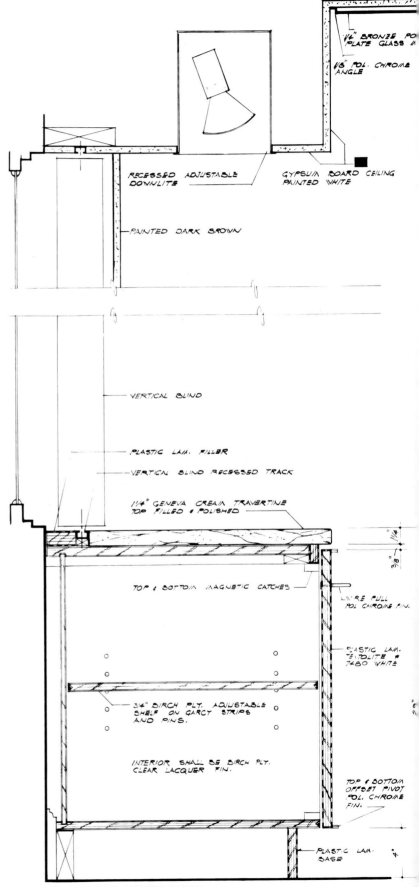

COUNTER AND CEILING DETAIL

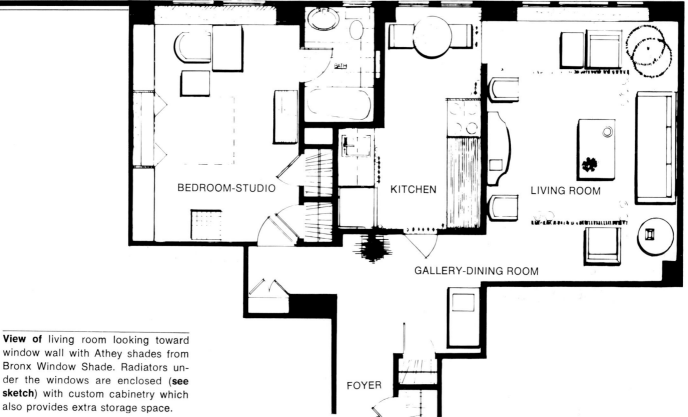

View of living room looking toward window wall with Athey shades from Bronx Window Shade. Radiators under the windows are enclosed (**see sketch**) with custom cabinetry which also provides extra storage space.

BEDROOM-STUDIO

BATH

KITCHEN

LIVING ROOM

GALLERY-DINING ROOM

FOYER

Flexibility is the Keynote

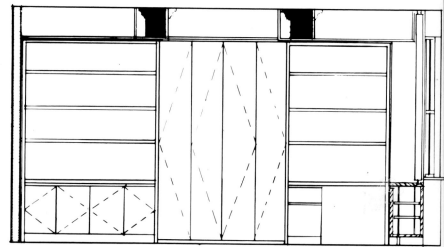

BED WALL ELEVATION

High Style in a Low Key

Or: The Case of the Reluctant Client

Yung Wang's residential interiors for a couple hesitant about hiring a professional designer

On the one hand there is Susan Browdy, a proficient potter and confirmed do-it-yourselfer who wasn't at all sure she ever wanted to work with an interior designer. Having moved, with her husband Joseph, from a small flat to a ten-room Manhattan co-op apartment she came to realize that the job of furnishing might be beyond her. But an outsider, she reasoned, never could understand her ideas. "I was afraid I'd end up with something totally overdone," she recalls, "To my mind, professional designers were associated with showrooms and magazines."

And on the other there is interior designer Yung Wang, who really wasn't sold on working with residential clients. For many years associated with leading architectural/design firms he had become accustomed to handling big-budget commissions for corporate interiors, and had come to like the impersonal aspects of contract work. The prospect of wasting time with cheeseparing or arbitrating family squabbles did not appeal immensely.

Hardly a cast of characters preordained for a spontaneous meeting of minds, but meet they did—through mutual friends—and inevitably talk turned to the new apartment. Susan Browdy,

whose pottery had piled up under furniture and on floors, knew she needed display space for her finished works. And her husband, a lawyer, wanted facilities for business entertaining. More to the point: both finally had come to accept that they had to have professional help to translate their objectives into reality.

In preliminary talks with Wang it was agreed that the proportions of the spaces, in a fine 1929 building, required no improvements or alterations. Main targets for action, according to the designer's subsequent plan, were [not necessarily in order of priorities]: to treat lighting—both natural and artificial—as an integral part of overall design; to make a couple of "strong statements" and to underplay

decorative applications otherwise; and additionally, to infuse colors and "a certain amount of sophistication."

Wang drew up working plans, but instead of progress there followed delay. Susan explains: "What happened was: those plans scared me. I couldn't relate them to the apartment, and I spent the summer sitting on them. The thought of giving my home to someone else to do still didn't seem right." Then came September, and renewed awareness that the job was too big to be handled by neophytes. "I was having second thoughts," Susan resumes, "when Joe said, 'We've hired a professional, let's go ahead.' So finally we did."

At this point Wang implemented the program, devising window treatments

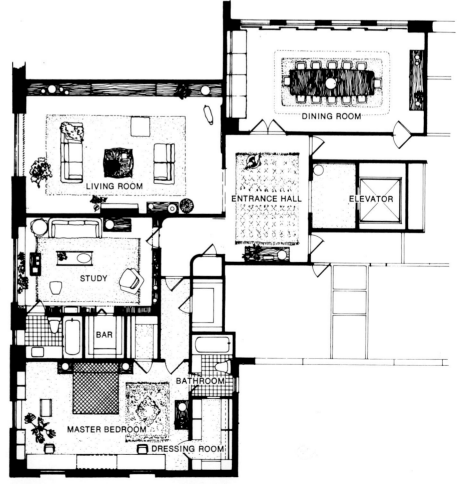

DINING ROOM

LIVING ROOM

ENTRANCE HALL

ELEVATOR

STUDY

BAR

BATHROOM

MASTER BEDROOM

DRESSING ROOM

High Style in a Low Key

to control excessive sun glare and installing concealed lighting behind all blinds so as to obliterate "black holes" at nighttime. He created his "strong statements," exemplified in the living room by the almost 30-foot-long display case/bar unit of lacquered white oak, internally lit and mirror-lined to show off the pottery samples and to effect a pivotal point of interest. In the foyer, another note of emphasis comes from the 17th-century Tibetan carved chest.

Believing that retention of some old things adds character, Wang had no objection to keeping intact the sofas and dining table brought along from the client's previous residence. ("I enjoy adapting things," he says, "often the old emerges looking better than the new.") For the bedroom he modified chests of drawers by removing the legs and topping the units with a counter. Elsewhere built-in shelving houses additional pottery displays, and colors create realms of individuality: deep rust in the dining room, slate blue in the hallway, soft putty in the bedroom. A banquette was installed along one wall in the dining room to accommodate business guests invited for cocktails, and the study also was planned to be appropriate for entertaining.

Characteristically, Wang refrained from over-decorating the spaces or from adding extraneous pieces. Thus,

for example, he omitted the customary console table behind the sofa, reasoning: why do something simply because everyone else always does it? Susan Browdy, for her part, contributed only items which have special meaning for her, such as the pottery, pictures done by friends, rugs and some accessories picked up during travels.

As for the total experience of working with a professional designer, looking back Susan says: "About a third through the job, as I began to see things happen, I knew that I could relax. Yung completely understood my taste after all, and his judgment always proved right." [Just one specific instance: she had suggested shelves for the dining room, but Wang recommended banquettes as supplying the wanted "softening" touch. His solution was the correct one, the clients agree.] Joe Browdy, too, is said to be delighted with the results.

The outcome is a vindication of Wang's design philosophy which he boils down to a simple dictum: "Appropriateness for the people involved is what matters most." Admittedly not a trend-setter or creator of fantasy stagings (these, he says, are fine for restaurants or discos but not for residences), he has given the Browdys that which suits and pleases.

In spite of the unpropitious beginning, a happy ending for all. **M.G.**

PRECEDING SPREAD

Focal point in the living room is the internally illuminated mirror-lined display/bar unit, made of lacquered white oak and nearly 30 feet long, which holds pottery samples made by Susan Browdy. Seating pieces were brought along from the previous residence, as was the wood-inlay coffee table. At left is an old Chinese blanket chest of ebony; on the table, accessories bought by Yung Wang in Bangkok; and on the floor, right, a pottery piece by Betty Woodman.

OPPOSITE PAGE

Study/guest room, (top photo) also used for business entertaining, contains rug from Tunisia, pottery by Susan Browdy, antique quilt and Indian work basket.

By deleting the legs of brought-along chests of drawers, Wang created a contemporary storage unit in the bedroom **(lower photo)**. The quilt was made by Susan Browdy; the drawings are by Anna Siok.

LEFT

Although outside the camera's range, a wall-long banquette opposite the bar unit provides facilities for business entertainment at cocktail time. Wang found the ceiling fixture, now available through other lighting sources, in Manhattan's Chinatown.

A Texas Trilogy

James Foy of Boswell-Foy Associates designs a residence for easy living, effortless entertaining, and enjoyment of the arts

James ("Tonny") Foy, who had designed the interiors of a house and offices for clients Mr. and Mrs. William F. Beckman before undertaking the illustrated residence in Fort Worth, seems to have developed a perceptive empathy for the owner-occupants' tastes and living habits. Explaining that the Beckmans both work "in a semi-retired way," he notes: "Everything about them is very natural—they entertain on short notice without stress or fuss, they love music and art, are open to new ideas, and really know how to enjoy life." The house, he indicates, is designed to reflect this joie de vivre, to provide a home base for entertaining, and to complement the clients' easygoing ways.

Thus there is no formalized approach to the design concept, and much of its appealing flavor comes from the pervading openness and visual linkage to the planting outdoors. Interior appointments, Foy remarks, rely on their interest not so much on color schematics as on their interrelationship of forms, textures and light. (In the main living area alone are found such diverse-surface materials as woods, willow, canvas, steel and smooth suedes.) This absence of regimentation extends to the fireplace which is treated not as a pivotal point for furniture placements but rather "like a painting in

---

A boardwalk leads to the glass-lined entry/breezeway of the house whose separate wings are connected by a bridge.

Living room, seen also on the following spread, is topped by three large skylights framed by sarsparilla wood paneling. Flooring is of diagonally laid oak.

Photographer: Jaime Ardiles-Arce

A Texas Trilogy

The owners' predilection for casual living as well as love for music and art are reflected in the design of the multi-function living room. Visible paintings are by John Z. Thomas, head of the art department at Hanover (Ind.) College; antique rugs, seen here and throughout the house, were collected by the clients during world travels.

a room." From a usage viewpoint, the living room is intended for widely varying activities and consequently contains a desk area, grand piano, facilities for film showings, and ample space for guest groups engaged in conversation.

Mrs. Beckman's comments about the interiors are as to-the-point as the overall planning concept: "It's a wonderful place for our casual way of life," she says, "and it serves our needs completely. Everything is useful and practical."

The two-bedroom house, by architect Al Komatsu, is made with sarsparilla wood ceiling detailing, multiple skylights, and diagonally laid oak flooring. Cabinetry was done by W. F. Beckman, the clients' son who acted as general contractor on the job. Not shown is the 75'-long indoor swimming pool at the basement level, the latter also giving rise to a two-story-high greenhouse which almost seems a part of the dining and kitchen areas. **M.G.**

A Texas Trilogy

1 **Glass-walled entry area** overlooks gardens in both directions.

1	2
	3

2 **Dining room** appears linked to two-story-high greenhouse rising from basement level (where indoor swimming pool, tucked beneath this area, also is located).

3 **Kitchen area** encompasses breakfast nook and sitting/reading room (with Victorian chair) to facilitate socializing while cookery is underway.

◀ **Master bedroom** accommodates desk and reading area. Round custom table is topped with granite.

◀ **Guest bedroom** contains heirloom bed, more than 100 years old, originally made with rope supports for feather mattress; and chests, about 25 years old, refurbished with paint. Framed artwork is by Josephana Roberosa; chairs and rug are clients' own.

Balancing Act

Connie Beale, ASID, satisfies the divergent tastes of a client couple in their new Houston townhouse

Balancing Act

THE SITE: a new two-story contemporary townhouse in Houston. The clients: a couple with divergent tastes; he, a partner in a large Houston-based architectural firm. The designer's task: to provide backgrounds and interior furnishings. The summary is simple; the actual project, however, was much less so. For designer Connie Beale walked a delicate balance in satisfying the tastes of both clients while also complementing the striking architecture.

As explained by Ms. Beale, the husband's preferences, given the nature of his work, lean towards clean contemporary spaces. The wife, on the other hand, favors more traditional elements such as antiques and Oriental rugs, and, says Ms. Beale, has tastes very similar to the designer's own. To please them both, she realized she had to "tailor the interiors for him, yet soften them so she was happy." Her selections, she continues, also had to provide a counterpoint to the glass and strong forms of the structure. In fact, the primary reason that she, an outside designer, was hired, was that the architect/client "was at a loss when it came to traditional interiors."

Structurally, the house is built around a central exterior courtyard, marked at the center with a fountain. On the first floor are a large living room, subtly divided into lounge seating and music/game areas; an adjacent dining room; the kitchen; and a gallery that leads one from the entry to the rear living/dining spaces. The living room is double height, and the illusion of expansive space is heightened by the windowed elevation that faces a terrace. Upstairs are the master suite, two bedrooms and a study.

Right: View of the living room with its double height ceiling and expanse of windows overlooking the deck. Antique items include the sarouk rug, the Oriental cocktail table, kilim fragments used for pillows, a small trunk used as an end table, a Japanese mirror, and the fire tools. The lithograph/collage is by Louise Nevelson.

Balancing Act

Ms. Beale's background selections—like the Mexican tile flooring throughout the first floor, woven grass cloth window treatments, and white walls—underscore the strength of the architecture while creating the neutral environment best suited to enhance the fine antiques and Oriental rugs. Some of these items were already owned by the clients. Others were newly purchased, but with an eye towards complementing those which existed. The result is a collection that looks as if it had been acquired over a period of years. We didn't want it to look as if they had amassed an instant collection, the designer comments. The only deviation from her pale neutrals scheme is in the dining room where the walls are painted a deep cordovan color. Furniture throughout, pleasantly sparse in concentration, is traditional without being formal. The clients are frequent hosts, and are most concerned with having their guests feel at ease.

Art works, purchased from local galleries, mark the start of an impressive collection of contemporary prints, paintings, and sculpture to harmonize with the antique objects. Artists represented are: Robert Motherwell, Laura Russell, Tom Sayre, Stephanie Cole, Dan Christianson, Dorothy Hood, Darryl Hughto, Alvaro Herran, Don Shaw, and Louise Nevelson.

The project was completed problem-free within a five-month time span. Total area measures approximately 5300 square feet. The general contractor was Pyramid Constructors, Inc.; the production architect was Charles Keith Associates.   **E.C.**

Above: View focusing on the piano and game area of the living room. A temple hanging, part of the owner's collection, is above an antique Chinese altar table. Other antiques are the Foo dog lamps, the Iroquois Indian potato stamp basket, the straw basket on the game table, and the horn box.

Below: Close-up view of the living room's main seating area. Above the fireplace is a lithograph/collage by Louise Nevelson.

Chapter 2

Weekend, Beach, Vacation Houses

*Patino-Wolf renovate and
design a Long Island residence*

The Quintessential Beach House

In short, this is everything a beach house should be. It is light, spacious and filled with what Bob Patino frankly calls "beautiful things" that reflect the client couple's flair for style. Yet it is also a pragmatic house whose simplicity has been studiously created to work for the clients—long-time friends of Patino and partner Vicente Wolf. Furnishings are flexible, easy to care for and "suitable, which," comments Patino, "is the key to good taste." (Hereafter quotes are attributed to the design team rather than to the individual.)

Given the finished project, one is hard-pressed to believe the designers' description of the original, purchased on a spur-of-the-moment decision. It was, they say, a nondescript box on stilts with only a small deck and no privacy from adjacent residences. Interiors were "pseudo-Mediterranean" in styling with wood flooring, dark wood cabinetry and a red brick fireplace built around a tubular metal chimney column. There was no differentiation between living and dining areas, and the second floor looked over a slight railing to the level below. Further, windows were marred with lattice work, and there were mouldings and strappings on walls and around frames. "It was a dark, dingy, depressing house," they say and confessed to doubts on their ability to make it meet the clients' standards. The clients, however, had no such qualms, and gave Patino and Wolf carte blanche as well as utmost trust.

The project, whose scope included almost total exterior as well as interior renovation, was one of evolution from the inside out. After stripping the background clean and painting it a "dead white," the designers based their first decision on selection of a material that could be extensively used and literally sponge-wiped clean. Their

Opposite and following spread: Living room views showing the restructured fireplace elevation and the way the space looks to the sea. Two-inch beige tile ("any other color shows the sand and dirt") was used extensively as a unifying element. All furniture, including customer built seating, is mobile. Photographs are by Irving Penn, Richard Avedon, Deborah Turbeville and Helmut Newton, and include a portrait of the wife and son by Avedon. **Above:** Exterior view shows newly created decks and portion of the boardwalk to the sea.

Photographer: Norman McGrath

The Quintessential Beach House

The Quintessential Beach House

Dining area with top of the dividing storage cabinet visible in the foreground and on opposite page. The table is an antique (whose top purposely has been left unfinished) purchased because the European clients believe that not everything should be contemporary. The driftwood "walking sticks" are found objects, and the dune grass was planted because the designers felt that flowers would look unnatural in this setting. The photograph is by Deborah Turbeville.

choice—a two-inch sand-colored tile that would surface floors, cabinetry and built-ins, and even furniture. All furniture ("none of which is serious for obvious reasons," they comment) is mobile. Metal carts work as consoles, bars or buffet servers. Custom seating, either single- or double-bed sized, is on large rubber wheels. Even the drum tables have a dual function; hinged tops open to provide storage for white terrycloth "fitted sheets" desiged as an easy cover option.

As expected, interior restructuring was extensive, with the designers making a strong graphic statement at one end of the public space. The living and dining rooms were separated by a double sided storage cabinet, surfaced with the pervasive two-inch tiles. Likewise, the fireplace and new adjacent wood storage unit are

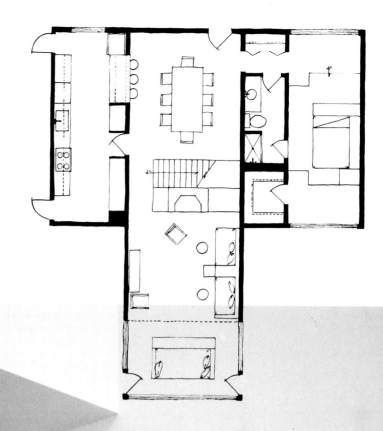

surfaced with the same material. The unsightly chimney tube was concealed within a large square column, and to balance this element, the stairwell was enclosed and upstairs balcony created. Fenestration was altered, and all lighting was recessed.

Once the interiors were so radically changed, the designers and clients became increasingly aware of the exterior shortcomings; now, that too needed redoing. Grey shingles were replaced with cedar planks that covered the stilts and took the structure down to the sand. The single small deck was enlarged, and the two side decks (pitched like lounge chairs to eliminate the need for furniture) were built. The designers even constructed a railed and lit-from-below "boardwalk" to the sea. Other exterior work included lighting instal-

The Quintessential Beach House

Below: One of two guest bedrooms. Sisal covers the floor, wall and bed base. The custom bed cover is white terry cloth designed like a fitted sheet.

Opposite: The master bedroom is as uncluttered as the rest of the house. The floor and bed platform have been raised to take maximum advantage of the view. The "headboard" doubles as storage cabinets.

lation and construction of a privacy wall that wraps around one side of the house to the front entrance. "There is really nothing of the original structure that is visible to the eye," they say.

As this project reflects Patino and Wolf, it also reflects its owners. For that is the way these designers profess to work. "People can't live in someone else's design philosophy," they say. "We always try to interpret a project through the client's eyes." And in this case, having designed three previous houses (including one on Fire Island) plus the husband's business quarters, the designers were familiar with the way the clients live. "We're part of their lifestyle," they say.   **E.C.**

Chic Beach

A Hampton, Long Island, residence designed by Michael de Santis

Chic Beach

Photographer: Mark Ross

"It's what I call chic beach," is Michael de Santis' terse description of the Hampton (Long Island) house designed for repeat clients. There was little thought of paring down or restricting furnishings to strictly utilitarian materials; a no-maintenance solution was not a prerequisite. These were clients clearly accustomed to a degree of luxury, and their second residence was to be no exception.

This is a new structure of contemporary idiom with four bedrooms and an open living/dining/kitchen area. Inside, de Santis made no spatial or structural changes. His work is based on selection of furnishings and finishes. As for personal preferences, the wife made only one definite request. She wanted pastels, and de Santis obliged. First, he had the ceiling of the "public" space painted a muted lavender color. Then he selected fabrics to further implement the theme. Pillow covers and upholstery material for the custom banquettes are handpainted cottons in pastel tones. Otherwise, neutrals prevail—denim covers on the wicker furniture, laminated raffia wall covering, pale wood floors with a custom colored off-white rug, and a cedar fireplace wall that replaces the original brick. When asked what about this project bears his personal stamp, the designer responds that it is his use of diverse textures. As a counterpoint to the neutral/natural materials mentioned, he used such slick elements as lacquer, plastic laminate and stainless steel for detailing.

While no interior alterations were effected, there was extensive building outside. A huge (53 by 75') cedar deck was added to accommodate a swimming pool and a cabana. No mere changing facility, the cabana also houses a sauna and bar facilities. "Here," says de Santis," is where the family really lives."   **E.C.**

Living room views (this page; opposite, above; preceding spread) show how the designer combines textures and materials to achieve a casual yet sophisticated tone. Elements designed by de Santis include the cocktail table with lacquer and stainless steel trim, the bar unit with lacquered straw and stainless steel finishes, the laminate and stainless steel dining table that expands to seat 14, and upholstered banquettes. The painting over the fireplace, by Claude Gaveau, is called "Chemin de la Plage." The general contractor for the project was DMK Construction.

Exterior view (opposite, below) shows the newly added 53 by 75' deck with pool and fully equipped cabana. The ceramic urns are designed and made by Lanzren; the fish are carved wooden pieces. Beyond is a view of the bay.

In the master bedroom, de Santis added a closet and custom designed the dresser unit and television cabinet. The end wall's mirror is bronzed.

Chic Beach

SAUNA

CABANA

BAR

POOL

NEW DECK, POOL AND POOL HOUSE

DOWN

EXISTING DECK

BEDROOM

DEN/GUEST

KITCHEN

MASTER BEDROOM

LIVING AREA

BEDROOM

BATH

LAUNDRY ROOM

DINING AREA

MASTER BATH

CLOSET

ENTRY

The house as seen from the swimming pool site.

Private Lives

*Ken Walker, with the informal assistance of his wife,
updates a historic island-retreat to suit the couple's personal tastes*

Kenneth Walker, AIA, president of Walker/Group, and his wife Mary bought the house which was to become their weekend-retreat in January of 1976. What sold him was the spacious garage for his racing cars and workshop. She was attracted by the manageability of the place. And both loved the idea of living in a building which traced its origins to the 19th century. Less than four months later, following work based on plans done by Walker and W/G partner Mark A. Kates, they had readied the dwelling for occupancy.

It is a very personal sort of house. Like some people it appears straightforward and simple on the surface, yet upon examination, reveals an interesting character shaped by varied forces. Even environment and heredity, to continue the analogy, played their part in exerting an influence.

For the building's history is, to the owners, a very real presence (which, as will be told later, affected the ensuing design treatment). Sited on an island about 100 miles east of Manhattan, the property dates back to 1893 when it served as a famous 300-room hotel. In 1910, after two fatal fires and subsequent rebuilding, it became a country club, and the structure now belonging to the Walkers was turned into a dormitory for golfers and guests. Only in 1923 was it purchased by a private family. It was then that the owners razed the roof and

lopped off corner, converting the whittled-down abode for staff use while themselves moving to a larger house on the grounds. Fifty-three years later, when the Walkers arrived, the smaller dwelling had been spun off as a separate property and structurally had been altered to approximate its present four-bedroom state.

As for the environs, this today is the Walkers' great source of pleasure. All living quarters are on the second level (the first is occupied by the garage and gym), and the house itself is situated about 50 feet above the out-lying water. Since windows on three sides face the ocean, it was agreed that nothing inside should compete with the proximity of nature. Thus interior architecture, furnishings and fixtures are treated as understudies to the star attraction.

In deference to the building's heritage, most altera-tions consisted of "a subtractive process . . . [confined to] paring away mistakes and past sins," Walker reports. And so, out went black-painted stairs, heavy window

View from dining area into living room and toward the bay. Furnishings throughout were chosen so as not to detract from outside views. The drawing is by Carol Anthony.

Photographer: Mark Ross

casements, an ungainly fireplace. Substituting for the latter is a Walker-designed unit, installed where inadequate cookery facilities formerly were found. The present kitchen, large and functional, takes the place of a quondam bedroom, and a dining ledge marks the spot of a taken-out wall. Enlargement of the master bathroom and restoration of hardware as well as window details were among other "anti-construction" changes.

Furnishings are classic and casual, mixing a few new purchases with good (but not precious or antique) old pieces. Uncharacteristically, Walker went easy on artworks. Only two pictures command focal attention, and both illustrate the property as it appeared in earlier days.

Looking from the kitchen to the living room the eye is drawn to a mezzo-print, processed and enlarged by Ken Walker, depicting the house as it was in 1910.

The main living area (stairway leads to garage and gym below) with dining area and kitchen in background. Hanging over the Walker-designed fireplace is an early 20th century needlepoint work.

Private Lives

Cast iron-and-wood bench from Finland was a house-warming present.

◀ **Part** of the original courtyard wall dating back to the start of the century.

Private Lives

That, on the face of it, wraps up the story. But since Ken Walker acted in the unaccustomed role of project designer as well as client, sharing decisions with his wife; and since his reputation rests on a record of super-contemporary contract installations; knowing this, one has to ask: did his professional work habits encroach on the process of private and collaborative design? And, could similarly gratifying results have been achieved by a qualified outsider?

To the second query, Walker responds with a flat "no." The reason, he states, also explains why he avoids residential assignments generally: domestic interiors, he believes, should be totally and exclusively representative of their occupants. (Yes, even if this is done at the expense of "good design." Comfort and personal life styles, he suggests, rarely conform with pure aesthetics.) Besides, a stranger never could have been as conscious of the building's historical past. "You must remember," he elaborates, "I studied and taught architectural history before I turned to architecture and design."

As for his background of contract work, he admits that without his wife's influence he might have been tempted to follow his usual decisive way of more ambitious and complex design. Instead, he adopted a deliberate policy of relaxed give-and-take. "I learned to slow down," he relates, "which was hard for me because I have little patience. Mary, on the other hand, will take all the time to think about her selections until she is quite certain they are right." He speaks respectfully of her high taste, and notes that the color choices were hers entirely. The house, he concludes, is better for having benefited from her contributions.

Mary Walker, asked later to add her comments, confirms that the collaboration was unusual and that it required the establishment of some ground rules. They agreed if one or the other disliked a proposed ingredient, the offending element would be dropped automatically. But a showdown never developed. (There was, in fact, only one compromise: His hardware, in her finish.) Is she game for another joint project? Definitely. As it happens, after having spent all her married life in an apartment pre-designed by her husband, she now is looking forward to the imminent move to new and co-planned premises in the city. **M.G.**

Small drawings in bedroom are by Dinah Smith and Carol Anthony.

As He Likes It

*Davis B. Allen designs his weekend retreat
to suit his personal taste and casual living style*

Davis B. Allen, whose New York State weekend house is seen on these pages, is an associate partner and senior interior designer in the New York office of Skidmore, Owings & Merrill. He is also, in a manner of speaking, a bit of a maverick: a leading industry figure given to understatement, economy of words, and strict avoidance of trade cliches. No reference does one hear to concepts, theories, philosophies. Not even one mention, so help us, of color schematics, interdisciplinary relations, or maximized design impact.

Thus his report about the country retreat, about 90 miles from Manhattan, is straight to the point and stripped of rhetorical flourish. He recounts the background story, telling of having lived in a rented house nearby for several years. Eventually he bought a plot and decided to build. This marked the first time ever he had designed a house for himself but even so, he know unhesitatingly what he wanted most: plenty of space, a sense of privacy, and a minimum of maintenance.

To suit the rural surroundings, the structure he designed is built in the shape of a barn. (As if to draw a verbal picture, Allen elaborates: "You see: stand in the center [of the two-story living room], and you can pitch up the hay to either side [in the upper bedrooms].") Because painting seemed an unnecessary bother, the house is of bare cypress inside and out. Four white-lacquered doors provide the only contrasting accent.

Even as the house was being finished, Allen still had no preconceived ideas about the interior design. He didn't aim for any particular theme or style, and certainly had no intent to "decorate." Step one was to move in with a minimum of furniture: a couch, and a couple of tables. Then gradually, he augmented these basics with furnishings from his city residence and his family's home, mingling in some pieces he had designed with others he had purchased here and there. "I like to see things grow," he asides.

And so, Allen sums up, now he is settled in, surrounded by all his stuff. How's that again: *stuff?* By way of a reply he gestures vaguely, pointing in the direction of the photographs depicting statuary and paintings. Ah yes, he means his artworks? No? His collection, then? Acquisitions? [One knows better by now than to speak of *objects.*] Acquisitions, he allows, is the acceptable word, and while he doesn't exactly wax eloquent, one senses that here is a subject which to him has deep meaning. These are pieces he bought over the past 30-some years, he relates, many of them linked to design projects he has handled for SOM. As he searched for accessories and accent pieces—frequently selecting

A portion of the living room, looking toward the dining area, The partially painted wood figures, made in the Solomon Islands, were bought in Paris. Decoy from India is one of four placed over each of the main-level doors.

Photographer: Jaime Ardiles-Arce

As He Likes It

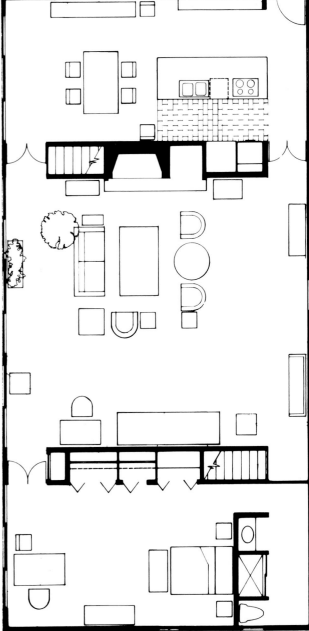

Three views of the 19-foot-high living room reveal varied acquisitions, most of them purchased by Allen in the course of his travels for SOM clients and including: rugs from Morocco; a Turkish lantern (the designer lived in Instanbul for two years while working on the Hilton Hotel); Spanish pitchforks with tree-branch tines shaped of continuous pieces (and placed in a focal position in lieu of an expensive, dramatic artwork); a tiger painted in India on cotton and purchased in Paris; clay lions from Mexico; 18th century carved fish from Japan; small figures and duck (on table) from Egypt; silver elephants from Angkor Wat; Spanish mirror; French botanical prints; Audubon lithographs; and more. The furniture consists of pieces designed by Allen (sofa, willow chairs, long table under tiger painting), or requisitioned from his family's home, or picked up here and there.

As He Likes It

prototoypes for adaptation—to be used in overseas hotels and other commercial installations, he developed the habit of purchasing samples for his own enjoyment. Now he has a wealth of varied objects ranging from trinkets to treasures, no two representing any one school but all providing pleasure to the owner. His "stuff," he concedes, is a very personal thing, of value because he likes it.

What the house does *not* contain is a separate dining room, simply because Allen never wanted one, and extra fireplaces (originally planned for the kitchen and bedroom where they were to have been built off the floor, at eye-level) because one (in the living room) proved quite sufficient for the time being. Similarly there were to have been two large seating groups, each with its own fireplace, but this, too, he decided he could do without. Nor is there an elaborate lighting system. Most artificial illumination comes from lamps made with vari-shaped bases, and in the kitchen there are down-positioned spots.

Externally the structure (1800 square feet on the main level, 900 on the second) looks to an unobstructed view of the countryside and the sea in the rear. The front, facing a public road, is sheltered with planting to assure privacy.   **M.G.**

Outdoor deck adjoining the living room, as seen also on the cover. The Solomon Island figures are thought to have been brought back by the Japanese during World War II. As for the iron furniture, this was liberated by Allen from his family.

Close-up of living room segment, near front door, focuses on old meeting-house pine bench, Hindu cow, Spanish mirror, and botanical prints.

Opposite: Kitchen/dining area contains custom chairs made in England, also oak burl-veneered table and cabinets designed by Allen, and French chairs of polished steel. By choice, cookery implements are kept on open shelves rather than in closed cupboards.

As He Likes It

Among the varied contents in Allen's bedroom (main level) are custom side tables and an English oak burl desk, 18th century American chest, a Spanish door used as a wall hanging, painted chickens from Haiti, and portrait of the occupant done by William F. Draper (who also painted cardinals and presidents, including John F. Kennedy).

Chapter 3

The dramatic effects that can be achieved with lighting

Tricks and Illusions

As architect/designer Cloud Rich tells it, his projects "emphasize form-continuity, lighting, illusions, texture, and aesthetically functional spatial structures." And if this Central Park West (Manhattan) apartment is any indication, the designer has given new definition to the term three-dimensional.

For background, this is a large 25th-floor apartment located in the building's southeast tower. Its chief asset is exposures on four sides; however, the small casement windows that existed precluded any sweeping views of the city. So, as the first order of business (and the only structural work required), Rich replaced them with tall vertical pivoting windows that, he says, "read as illuminated postcard views of Manhattan by night."

The space—designed in phases as funds became available—was to function as both residence and working facility for client Alma Daniels, who had left the business world to set up a counseling/referral self-improvement service for both individuals and groups. To go along with her "awareness" or "self-improvement" programs, she also had one room designed around an isolation chamber where the participant immerses himself into epsomsalted, body temperature water for a period of time purportedly to reduce stress.

Right from the entrance, one gets clues of the illusionary tricks that are to follow. Here, beams of light are projected through turning crystal prisms to create the changing light painting on the wall. The living room, given the client's requirements, had to function well for both small and large groups of people. To zone this large expanse into more intimate areas, Rich used a change in floor levels which also brings a sense of movement to the room. The area in front of the windows is raised two feet to the sill level, with part of this platform housing what Rich calls "a recessed people pit" for small groups to gather around a removable table.

One of the most intriguing aspects about this project is the pervasive technique called space painting, a concept that Rich says "wraps the design around three dimensions." The technique entails painting sections of a wall or ceiling to reflect structural changes on the

Cloud Rich uses innovative elements in the design of a Manhattan apartment to function as residence and working facility

Opposite, above: The designer's preoccupation with lighting is first seen in the entry foyer where crystal lighting creates a kinetic wall picture. Also the American folk art sculpture is carefully lit—from above by a spot fixture, from below by its lighted Plexiglas pedestal.

Opposite, below: This view of the living room facing the fireplace shows one example of the space painting technique. The ceiling over the platformed area and the fireplace elevation is painted white in contrast with the predominant salmon tone. The treatment, according to the designer, makes the mirror-lined fireplace appear to move forward.

Photographer: Jaime Ardiles-Arce

Tricks and Illusions

Overall view of the living room showing how the space painting and level changes help zone the room into areas with more
intimate scale. Just visible in the background is the "recessed
people pit" which is built into a section of the platform. The
uncovered windows, according to the designer, read as postcard views of Manhattan. The sculptures, early American folk
art, were part of the client's collection.

This page: The library is a small, irregularly shaped room (7 to 10½ feet wide, 14 feet deep) made to appear wider by horizontal bands of color—salmon, "barn" red and two mixed values of them. Mirrors also perceptually enlarge the room which works as a private office, consulting room and occasional guest room. Below the bookshelves another of the many "light boxes" highlights photographs.

Opposite: Bedroom views show a room divided into sectors for working/dressing and sleeping. The soffit over the desk/dressing table is the same height as the light fixture centrally located over the platformed bed cum storage unit. The focal point of the room, however, is the windowed elevation where Rich's infinity chamber is flanked by two large pivoting windows—this whole area presenting a somewhat surrealistic situation at night. As in the living room, the space in front of the windows is platformed to sill level.

Tricks and Illusions

floor level, or to make certain planes appear prominent or recessive. Space painting is used: in the living room where the ceiling sectors above the platform and the fireplace elevation are painted white as opposed to the predominant salmon tone; in the dining room where walls progress from white through pale taupe to the darker taupe matching the carpet, making the dark wall appear to recede; in the library where four horizontal bands based on shades of salmon, brick red and a combination of the two add a perception of width to the tiny room; and in the "isolation" room where color changes coupled with level changes establish two distinct zones.

Throughout the apartment, most of the furniture was custom designed for multi-function, and some of it designed to incorporate storage. In the living room, the chaise longue is sectional, allowing the two pieces to be detached and moved to other areas of the room. The banquette construction, in addition to providing traditional seating, offers extra space for guests to sit on its platformed surround. The dining table is a group of four laminate-topped surfaces on pedestals which can be grouped in various configurations. Some of the horizontal surfaces also work as light boxes. For example the clear and opaque Plexiglas cocktail table is lit from its base which casts a ring of light around the perimeter; an insert surface in the platform is lit from below to highlight a piece of early American folk art; and the wall-hung dining room shelf is lit from within. Likewise the furniture in the master bedroom was custom designed to zone the room into a dressing room/work area and also a central sleeping section where storage compartments are built into the platformed structure.

Although Rich's principal tricks of perception come from his space painting use of mirrors and lighting (all on rheostat-control and carefully placed to highlight a specific area or artwork), he has devised two other innovative treatments worthy of mention. In the living room, he lined the inoperable fireplace with mirror and placed lighted candles in glass holders to simulate a fire. In a cut-off corner between two windows in the master bedroom, he built an "infinity lightbox" lined with two-way mirrors. As seen from the bed, this expanse presents a slightly surrealistic situation with this "view to nowhere" flanked by city vistas. "The lightbox," says Rich, "is a metaphorical way of leaving the room."

Concluding, he states that this apartment quite definitely changes in feeling from day to night. There is a constant interchange, where during daylight hours the rooms themselves are dominant, but at night, the views from the exterior take over. **E.C.**

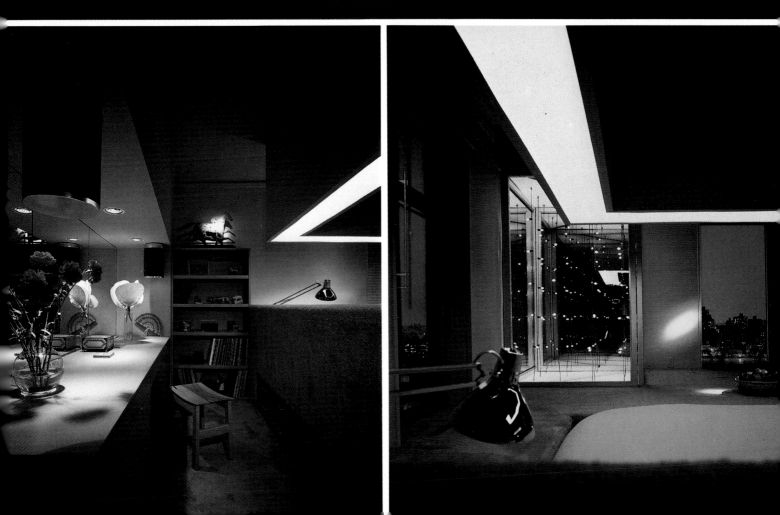

Switched-On Manhattan

Roger McKean Bazeley combines neon
with a bold color palette to fashion
an interior both dramatic and whimsical

A switch is flipped. And suddenly the skyline of Manhattan flashes across the living room wall as bright and radiant as a Broadway marquee. Like the real Manhattan cityscape, it shimmers and pulsates as electricity courses through its glass veins at hundreds of miles per second.

This is neon. It comes from the Greek word "neos" or new, and its light is produced by a gas that glows intensely when an electrical current is passed through it. And although discovered some 70 years ago, its potential as a source for interior lighting and architectural embellishment is just beginning to be realized. To most people, neon remains part of the roadside and urban glitter associated with motels, taverns, and Las Vegas casinos.

Fortunately, many designers and architects are recognizing neon's potential and rescuing it from its tainted image. Roger McKean Bazeley is one of them. To Bazeley, an interior designer who studied graphics and industrial design, neon is a natural. It was the perfect medium with which to create the mural for this Manhattan duplex apartment, and the slick contemporary interior his clients wanted.

The choice of the mural's subject matter—the Manhattan skyline—was not arbitrary. The young professional couple who bought the apartment had both gone to college in Manhattan and had moved back to the island to partake of its cultural vitality. But their apartment, located in a former Greenwich Village factory converted to cooperatives, had one major drawback—no view. The windows faced squarely into adjacent buildings. (Admittedly, this is an encumbrance which many New Yorkers grudgingly put up with.) But Bazeley's solution—to bring the city's panorama inside—is more than simply "the next best thing." For it gives the interior the vibrant and slightly surreal color effects that only neon, and not post-card-perfect vistas, can achieve.

Before Bazeley went to work, the interior was already a cleanly articulated space. The fascia which delineates the kitchen gives it a structural identity while allowing easy and informal access to the living area. The balustraded stairway, which zig-zags to the second level, also imparts a crisp geometry.

However, the designer's choice of furniture and his color palette help define this geometry, and in doing so, give the interior real graphic punch. The colors are, by his own admission, high-tech and industrial. Against a neutral grey carpet and white walls, Bazeley has juxtaposed cobalt blues and magentas. And he is not afraid to combine colors which one might presume would clash. Witness the primary red cabinets in the guest room and dining area juxtaposed to, respectively, the magenta carpeting and wall. Oddly, it works.

All of these elements are knit together in a way that preserves the apartment's inherent openness and continuity. "I tried to give each area its own identity and function, without relinquishing a sense of flow and movement from one area to another," explains the designer. But it is Bazeley's ability to articulate this "flow" through color and neon light that gives the interior its rhythm and visual excitement.   **J.T.**

Photographer: Mark Ross

Opposite: Designed by Bazeley, the neon mural of the Manhattan skyline has powerful graphic impact, and the cool blue light it casts over the room softens the cobalt blues and magentas of the furniture.

Subtle Spaces

A Manhattan cooperative totally transformed by Arthur Ferber

"The apartment was a horror—a real disaster. It looked like a tenement," Arthur Ferber recalls his original reaction to this East Side Manhattan co-operative. But Ferber, not one to shy from challenge, accepted the commission and transformed what had been a small, badly cut-up space into a well organized apartment alive with subtle colorings, metallic lacquer finishes, and dramatic lighting effects.

The project was one requiring extensive architectural alteration; surface decor was secondary. Yet before a single plan was made, Ferber conducted detailed interviews to find out how his client lives. He learned, first of all, that this was to be an evening apartment. He also learned that she entertains frequently and loves to cook, yet does not like being isolated from guests. So, a redo of the kitchen was the point of departure. Ferber cut a pass-through into the wall dividing the kitchen and living room; this linked the two areas.

In the entry foyer, he created a dramatic chiaroscuro effect with pools of light and pale green (termed sea foam) walls contrasting with deep magenta lacquered screens. More than mere decoration, however, the screens are on top and bottom tracks, and slide away to reveal doorless closets.

In the living room, approximately 13' x 23', Ferber mirrored end walls from floor to ceiling so that furniture between the two planes would appear to float. Here, his splendid palette of "sea foam," pale grey, magenta and black comes together with furniture, lighting and views into the adjacent kitchen and hallway.

Lighting in the living room and kitchen is based primarily on low-voltage incandescent sources in track fixtures. Double circuitry provides flexibility while pink filters in both areas provide mood. Uplight fxtures are used for accent lighting.

Of seven months' duration, the project was problem-free, which Ferber attributes to meticulous planning and background-in-the-arts discipline. Formerly a painter, he professes to see the completed project in his mind's eye before a single plan is put into work. "From that vision, it's simple to get it to the right point." **E.C.**

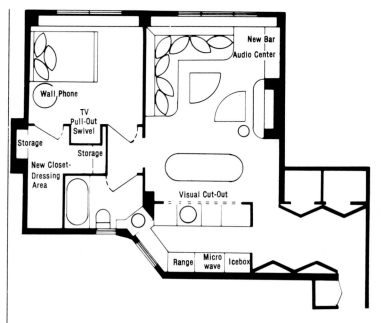

Photographer: Jaime Ardiles-Arce

Painting with Light

A Los Angeles residence by Hendrix/Allardyce

Painting with Light

To make maximum use of a small area, Hendrix/Allardyce built a triangular storage unit in the family room to house television (facing the seating) and stereo equipment. The all-neutral palette is accented by the custom colored carpet.

Photographer: Sheldon Lettich

For this residence in Los Angeles, Hendrix/Allardyce coupled extensive architectural remodeling with furnishings selection and design to produce the pictured results.

Originally, says Thomas Allardyce, this was a "simple '50-ish style house" on two levels. On the upper or main level, the designers concentrated on opening up what had been badly cut-up space so that the living room, dining area and master bedroom would read as a unified image. They also cleaned up the background shell by removing some of the decorative features like "inferior wood cabinetry," says Allardyce. On the lower level, which originally housed only a play room and the garage, Hendrix/Allardyce incorporated a new addition built into the hillside to accommodate a guest room and bath.

The color palette throughout the house is based on neutrals with accents of bright color in the pillows and carpet detailing. Most of the color in the project comes from two sources—the focal-point paintings by George Kleiman and the lighting that was specially designed to produce colors complementary to those of the artworks. The system, Allardyce explains, is based on theatrical fixtures with colored gels that have been adapted to fit into lighting tracks. Its flexibility comes from the 200 color possibilities available. And, aside from the obvious, another feature of this lighting system, according to its designer, is that visually the colored lights decrease the volume of the walls. The result is that the entire space appears to be larger. All of the lighting is remote-controlled, and can be programmed for bright or dim atmospheric effects.

Most of the furniture is custom designed, including upholstered seating; the cocktail table, a filled travertine top with recessed lighting on a brass base; the triangular cabinet housing television and stereo equipment in the play room; and the master bedroom furniture.

E.C.

Preceding spread and opposite, above: The main level was restructured so that the living and dining areas would be a continuous space. The lighting is a specially designed system using theatrical fixtures and gels to duplicate the colors in the painting by George Kleiman.

Opposite, below: The master bedroom, on the main level, continues the living room theme with the same carpet, color palette, related forms and painting by George Kleiman.

Chapter 4

Architectural re-shaping of spaces

An Apartment of Ideas

Architects Gwathmey Siegel rebuild a Manhattan cooperative

Although hard to believe from photographic evidence, this Manhattan cooperative apartment was originally a traditional cellular residence with rectangular rooms connected by a typical maze of corridors. Architects Charles Gwathmey and Robert Siegel soon changed that. They completely restructured the interior space, approaching the project much as if they were building a house from start.

"This is the first apartment we treated as if we were working from scratch," begins Gwathmey on a theoretical note. "The difference is that in a house, we have control of all forms. In an apartment, the container is given." The object here, he continues, was to reclarify this given container in terms of a newly established spatial flow. "Our intent was to treat the space as a solid modulating sculpture that changes from every viewpoint."

Only the elevator lobby and the core columns were maintained. Otherwise, rooms were combined to form large flowing spaces, many of them defined by the architects' signature glass block or curved walls. A living room and dining room were combined to form a related area, partitioned only by a custom built buffet unit. A master suite comprised of bed chamber and den replaces two smaller and separate rooms. The entire kitchen area was opened up to include a breakfast room; it had been a series of servants' quarters, kitchen and pantry. Traditional long hallways were restructured to fulfill a dual purpose. Examples are the gallery, just off the entrance, and the children's play area, formed by incorporating a former servants' hall into a just-widened corridor. Further, ceilings in what Gwathmey calls "transition zones" and in the corridors were dropped to 7' 6"; elsewhere ceilings are 9 feet high. A close study of the before and after floor plans better explains the extent of the spatial renovation.

Two views of the gallery which leads from the entrance to the living and dining areas. One entire wall, the longest continuous wall in the apartment, is mirrored to reflect the warmth implied by the oak flooring and cabinetry, as well as emphasize the sculpture. Here is the initial use of the muted color palette that is repeated throughout the apartment.

Photographer: Norman McGrath

The child's bedroom (top photo) is actually smaller in size than it was in the original plan, since space was "borrowed" from it to create part of the playroom. However, the built-in furniture makes it appear larger than it was initially.

The playroom (lower photo) was created by incorporating a corridor, "borrowed" space from two bedrooms, and a servants' hall (see plans). The built-in furniture and cabinetry eliminate clutter, and lend a ship-like appearance to the space. At the end of the space is the salmon colored niche, shown in closeup on the opposite page.

An Apartment of Ideas

AFTER

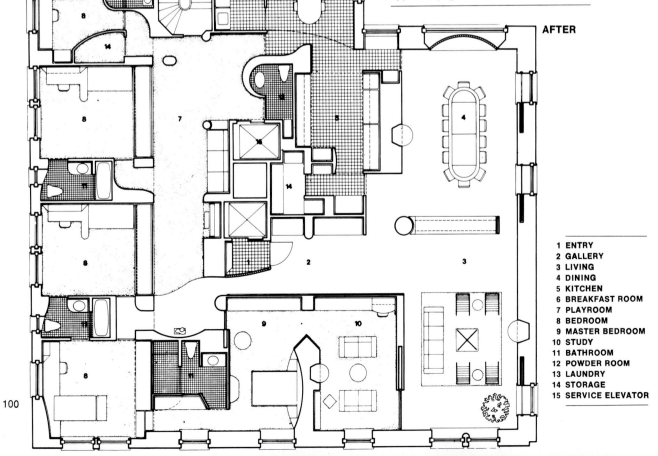

1 ENTRY
2 GALLERY
3 LIVING
4 DINING
5 KITCHEN
6 BREAKFAST ROOM
7 PLAYROOM
8 BEDROOM
9 MASTER BEDROOM
10 STUDY
11 BATHROOM
12 POWDER ROOM
13 LAUNDRY
14 STORAGE
15 SERVICE ELEVATOR

Views of the dining room. Here is the best illustration of the dark and light grey walls and how they intersect. Separating without totally dividing the dining area from the adjacent living room is a custom built two-sided unit. On the dining room side, it functions as a buffet server; on the living room side, there is storage for books and stereo equipment. The dining table is a custom design of oak with an antique verde marble top. Gwathmey refers to the curved glass block end-wall in historical terms—as an "apse that terminates the whole sector" (see plan). The large painting is by Roy Lichtenstein.

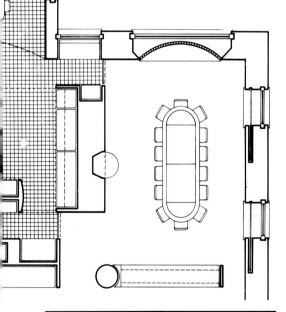

An Apartment of Ideas

An Apartment of Ideas

Although the apartment is consistent within the Gwathmey Siegel oeuvre, it does represent a considerable step forward in the use of color, richer materials and intricacy of detailing. According to Gwathmey, this is the first time that the architects departed from a basic black-and-white no-color scheme to experiment with color. And experiment it was since, "we were never sure of the color until the end. I was there every day with the painters while the work was in progress," he says.

This is not to say that the architects went wild with color. The palette is expectedly subtle— white; dark and light grey also acting as neutrals; pale salmon, lavender, and avocado, secondary hues that are "part of an intuitive pastel palette harmonizing with grey." Colors are applied as follows. Higher ceilings are white; the lowered "transition" ceilings are dark grey. East/west walls are dark grey, while elevations at right angles to them are light grey. Yes, the colors are aesthetically pleasing and lend "an element of surprise" to the space. But Gwathmey and Siegel rarely make choices strictly for aesthetic reasons, and this is no exception. The interplay of dark and light imply a structural function, giving sharp definition to every intersection. Further, Gwathmey explains, this positioning of dark and light was planned in much the same way that they would plan fenestration in a house being built from scratch. Here, however, the dark and light areas as articulated by the windows were already given. The pastel colors, used to accent columns and particular wall sectors, establish "a sense of vertical volume as they intersect with the white ceiling plane."

Just as the use of color is meticulously detailed, so is the custom built work, which throughout the apartment eliminates the need for quantities of traditional free-standing furniture. The cabinetry is sleek and streamlined, giving the interiors the uncluttered look of a luxury liner. Throughout the cabinetry is of oak, as are the floors.

Aside from oak, mirror is the most frequently used material. "Mirror is always thought to be a cold material," says Gwathmey, "but this is not so at all." He explains that it is really a neutral material taking on the value of the materials it reflects. And here, since it reflects so much oak, it really intensifies a feeling of warmth. It also makes a space appear less static since "it destroys opacity" and reflects the movement of people.

Perhaps Gwathmey's conclusion best explains the thought processes behind the very attractive project. "The apartment is simultaneously very livable, yet so much of it is an idea. The subtleties force one to be acutely perceptive of this built-in environment. Throughout, there is a constant sense of mystery and discovery." □

One of the most dynamic aspects of the apartment is the multiplicity of views provided by the long gallery. From the vantage point here, one looks into the master bedroom at a photograph by Edward Steichen and down the gallery to a painting by Ellsworth Kelly. The dark grey column is part of the grey-plus pastel color palette.

Opposite: The bedroom (above) and den (below) comprise the master suite created from what had been two separate rooms. Again, almost all furniture is built in, even to the "cyclops eye" holding the television.

Defining the Qualities of Space

*Balanced scale and functional delineations
distinguish a Manhattan duplex by Bray-Schaible Design, Inc.*

The old saw about the comparative worth of picture and words cuts neither way when it comes to the Manhattan duplex covered on these pages. Only first-hand viewing, in its full perspective, can reveal the project's total effect.

"Total" being the decisive term. For as designed by Robert Bray and Michael Schaible, the interior's impact depends on an inseparable intermeshing of custom components, artworks, exterior views and overhead mirroring, all balanced and scaled to enhance the sweeping expanse. It's as if each element, far from filling up volume, contributed a measure of spaciousness.

Queried first about the unusual stone formations shown prominently in the lead-off photographs, the designers indicate that these were not intended as a design statement. (Nor, it transpires, do they dominate the space when seen in the context of the entire environment.) Instead, quite simply, they resulted from the necessity of dividing and delineating the 1400-square-foot living area into functional segments. Thus the pyramid-reminiscent forms of Kasota stone are "a whimsical device" which, moreover, afforded the irresistible opportunity of using this beautiful ivory-like material. The clients, a well-traveled couple occupying the New York residence only part of the year, are said to be equally enthusiastic about the arresting treatment.

Slanted on the outside and narrow-ledged to avoid any semblance of massive bulk, the stonework partially frames two seating enclaves and shelters "very soft, warm and intimate" banquettes fronted with tables. Comfort further extends to the more conventional dining area where seating is provided by lounge chairs and where the table, as holds true for the smaller models, is below standard height. During large parties, it is re-

Two views from opposite ends of the entry section and one from the window wall **(opposite, below)** show slanted exteriors of Kasota stone seating enclosures. Stonework dimensions are 52″ high, 24″ across base, 4″ wide at the top and one or two feet at short side segments.

Photographer: Jaime Ardiles-Arce

Close-up of banquette with control panel for sound system **(above)** facing dining group **(opposite),** set on Chinese rug, in living area. Since the emphasis is on casual comfort, all tables are below standard height and lounge chairs take the place of more formal seating. During parties, up to 30 people can enjoy sit-down meals eaten off solid surfaces. In the background, topping the television/sitting space, are three beam-scored mirrors, placed in recesses created by taking out portions of the false ceiling, which pick up exterior views and appear to raise the height. Between the windows is a sliding panel useable as projection screen. Visible artworks include Chinese Buddha and T'ang horses.

Defining the Qualities of Space

Defining the Qualities of Space

ported, people form a kinetic pattern as they move about, sit down, and regroup into clusters of conversation.

As for the overall design approach, the prime consideration was to take advantage of the Central Park exposures and accordingly, to gut and "open up the entire periphery" on the main level. Windows now are unobstructed, focally visible from any location, and, in some instances, seemingly accentuated where walls have been thickened slightly. Grilles atop sills conceal heating and air conditioning.

Perhaps as important as opening up the space was counteracting the potentially oppressive effect of 8'-low ceilings. To this end Bray/Schaible rerouted the overhead air conditioning and, in two locations, replaced segments of the false ceiling with mirrors. The resulting effect is astonishing. Not only do the reflected mirror-images give the illusion of added elevation but also, they seem to reach out laterally to bring inside parts of the exterior park views. Similarly comprehension-defying (to a neophyte) are the workings of the chair-side panels and pantry-based master control board which

Master control board for the complex sound system is located in pantry and monitors AM/FM radio, TV, recordings and tapes throughout the duplex apartment. Stereo equipment and bar supplies are in cabinets.

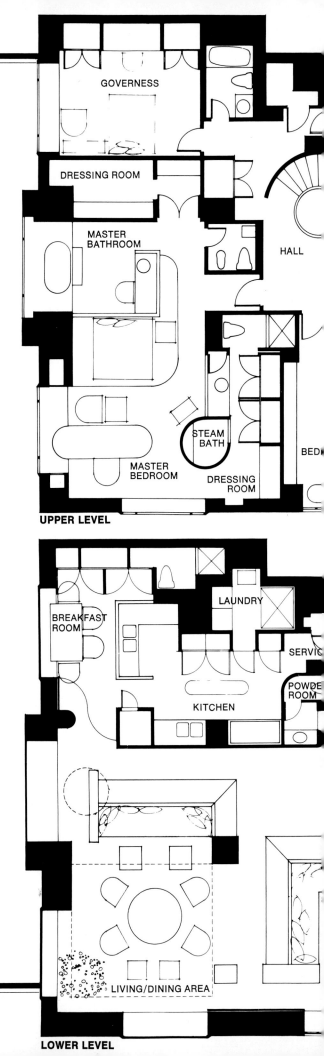

UPPER LEVEL

LOWER LEVEL

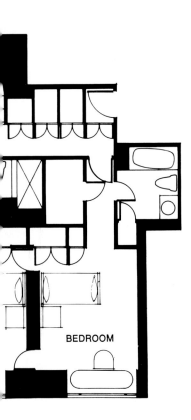

BEDROOM

Above: Level-linking stairway continues use of Kasota stone and, behind columnar curve, shelters a wash-up basin.

Below: View from breakfast room to dining area illustrates grille-topped window sill which conceals heating/air conditioning, and 5'-diameter overhead mirror which picks up dining-segment reflection. Figures and horses are Chinese antiques.

FOYER

OOM

BUTLER'S ROOM

PANTRY/BAR, STEREO

The client couple's master bedroom, seen from two angles, contains large table of Kasota stone. Her bathroom is behind 6′ 8″-high carpeted wall; his behind the partition next to the column which, in turn, encloses a steam bath.

Defining the Qualities of Space

regulate AM/FM radio stations, television channels, two record players, cassettes, and reel-to-reel tape decks.

Linking the two apartment levels is a curving staircase which continues the use of Kasota stone from dividers and flooring below to major design applications above. The master bath (not illustrated), with its own large window exposure, is made of the pink-cast substance entirely, as is the table in the bedroom. Here a previously walled-over window was opened up, again to make exterior views part of the interior schemes. Exceptionally appealing, too, are the two children's quarters, identically furnished except for the mirror-backed barre in the girl's room and book stacks in the boy's. Doors flanking either side of the connecting wall provide access for shared activities. **M.G.**

Complex Simplicity

A Manhattan apartment by Adam Tihany

A t first glance, it looks so simple. Colors are black or off-white. Furnishings are restricted to a few bold forms, as are artwork and accessories. Nothing is superfluous. But, first impressions, as we know, often deceive. For behind this serene facade lies a complex process of thought, selection, elimination and detailing. This type of solution leaves no room for error.

The apartment, according to its designer Adam Tihany, is a perfect illustration of the single tenet he holds when it comes to residential design. "I provide only the architectural elements and the basic furnishings," he says. "I believe in giving the client a neutral, comfortable environment in which he can express himself—in which he can add or subtract elements without fear that he will disrupt the design." Thus, the client and Tihany were in perfect accord; the client's sole request was that the apartment not look as if it had been "decorated" by someone else.

The apartment is a 1000-square-foot, two-bedroom rental unit in one of Manhattan's newer highrise structures. At the start its plan was similar to any other residence of this ilk. On entering the space, Tihany explains, one found "doors leading everywhere." He removed them all. Then, he widened the foyer by about two feet, and gave a focal point to its end with a lattice and frosted glass door, its design recalling that of a shoji screen.

A less-than-full-height partition curves around to the main living/dining space where one discovers this element to be the back of a seating banquette that also doubles as a guest bed. Two additional sofas, an end table, and the client's existing lacquered cocktail table (which rises to work as a secondary dining surface) are the only other pieces of furniture in the room. The stereo system and television are neatly housed within the wall which Tihany extended and curved around to the adjacent dining room.

The entry was considerably widened and restructured so that a single shoji-like door separates the private sector from the living/dining area on the other side of the curved partition. A lacquered shelf was designed for the eventual display of objects, should the client wish to add them; the art is by Israeli artist Benni Efrat. The general contractor was Mariano Construction Co.

Photographer: Mark Ross

Complex Simplicity

Complex Simplicity

The ceiling is painted black because, says Tihany, "everything else is light." At night, it disappears, giving the space an infinite quality—as if the room were open to the sky. For this reason, the doors were designed as full-height openings within the walls, which at night are the only perceived boundaries to the space.

The private sector of the apartment lies behind the shoji-like door. What were originally two bedrooms were restructured to form a conjoining bedroom and library. The two are separated by a sliding panel whose design is the same lattice and glass treatment. So acute is Tihany's attention to detail that he had the panel's grid duplicate that of the custom storage system (not visible) he built to face it. Other examples of this penchant for detail include the closets, built in the European manner with a drawer for everything, and all visible hardware.

The project was completed in ten weeks for $80,000 all-inclusive, a figure considered low for the amount of work involved. "But," says Tihany whose budgets are usually much higher, "I did it because the client is a friend." **E.C.**

Preceding spread: The living room is a study in pared-down simplicity without its being in any way stark. The custom banquette, which incorporates an end table, works as a single bed. The cocktail table, existing, can be raised to function as a secondary dining surface. The artwork is by Jasper Johns and Roy Lichtenstein; the glass works are by Ettore Sottsass for Vistosi.

Opposite: View from the library into the bedroom. Both of these areas are continuations of the pure background statement established in the living area. The grid of the sliding glass door duplicates that of the storage system (not visible) that it faces. The window coverings in these two rooms are black-out shades, operated by a remote-controlled sonic device.

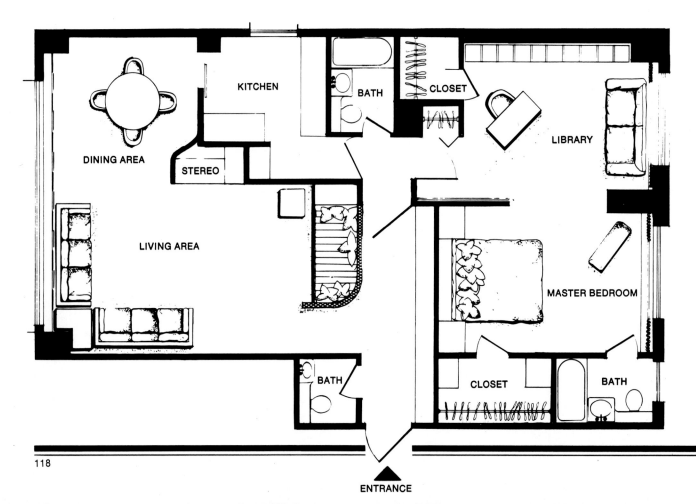

DINING AREA

KITCHEN

BATH

CLOSET

LIBRARY

STEREO

LIVING AREA

MASTER BEDROOM

BATH

CLOSET

BATH

ENTRANCE

Understanding Understatement

Patino/Wolf's design of a Manhattan cooperative

It takes a certain savoir-faire to be able to pull off an interior based on subtleties. Too much, and the message is lost. Too little, and the project borders on boredom. But there was no such chance that Bob Patino and Vicente Wolf would err in either direction; they are masters of the genre. Testimony to the fact is this U.N. Plaza (Manhattan) cooperative, an amalgam of harmonius textures, forms, and colors.

Although the three-bedroom apartment, in a building famed for its views, was basically well laid out with distinct up-front public/entertaining areas and rear private quarters, the designers did make some spatial alterations. "We needed to re-evaluate the space so that it would best function for entertaining," explains Patino, who acted as spokesman during our interview. As it had heretofore existed, it fell somewhat short of its potential.

Originally, there had been separate closed-off areas to function as living room, dining room and smaller sitting room or den. Patino/Wolf thought the divisions unnecessary. So did the clients. The space was opened up to provide, on one hand, a rather grand entertainment sector. Yet, on the other hand, it is also a series of interconnected intimate enclaves, created by the judicious placement of elements.

Structural work also included rounding the exposed support columns to pave the way for a background that would eventually have no sharp edges despite its contemporary genre. A free-standing divider, somewhat like an expanded column in form, was built to separate the small den from the adjacent and more formal living room (see plan). This element is an intriguing one. On one face, it frames the Louise Nevelson work within a niche that is lit from above. On the opposite side that fronts the den, it houses an exposed music system and television/video equipment.

In selecting the finishes, color palette and furnishings, the designers had a single guideline from the client. The apartment, says Patino, "was to be light and airy with nothing obstructing the views." In the words of the client, it was to resemble "a glass of champagne."

Thus the clue to the finishes and colors. Flooring in the front public areas is travertine with carpet defining the three function areas. Walls are painted ivory, tinted with casts of pink or peach, and the den's rear wall is an apricot tone in a textured finish. One only becomes aware of these tonalities, an effect described as "undulating" by Patino, in the evening hours. During the day, the sun bleaches the background to a uniform off-white color.

Virtually all furniture elements are custom designed and situated to give architectural definition to the space. For example, a marble-topped console with overhead lighting soffit leads on from the entry to the public area. And opposite, the same marble tops the frame for the living room banquettes, making a strong statement of symmetry. Seating throughout is based on rounded forms. Covers are neutral toned, yet material

Left: "What you see here is a sense of balance and symmetry," says Patino of the entry. The form of the marble-topped console with overhead light soffit is repeated opposite as the frame for the living room banquettes. The free-standing partition suggests the boundary of the den. The rug is an antique silk Tabriz; the phtograph on the console is by Irving Penn.

Opposite: View of the stepped-up living room with the Nevelson work recessed in one face of the free-standing partition. The nesting tables, lacquered with eggshell inlays, are by Jean Dunand. They satisfied the clients' desire for something from the Deco era yet without being obviously so.

Photographer: Peter Vitale

Views of the living room with its full height wrap-around windows. Here, one sees the harmonious interplay of selected materials. The same marble used for flooring and the consoles in the foyer tops the banquette frames and is used for the oversized cocktail table. The suede that covers the chairs and pillows was specially imported by the designers from Italy. The Henry Moore sculpture, purchased by the designers for the clients, sits on a revolving base so that it can be seen from a variety of angles in the overall space. A small, albeit major work was purposely selected so as to not overwhelm the room. All furniture was custom designed.

Understanding Understatement

Understanding Understatement

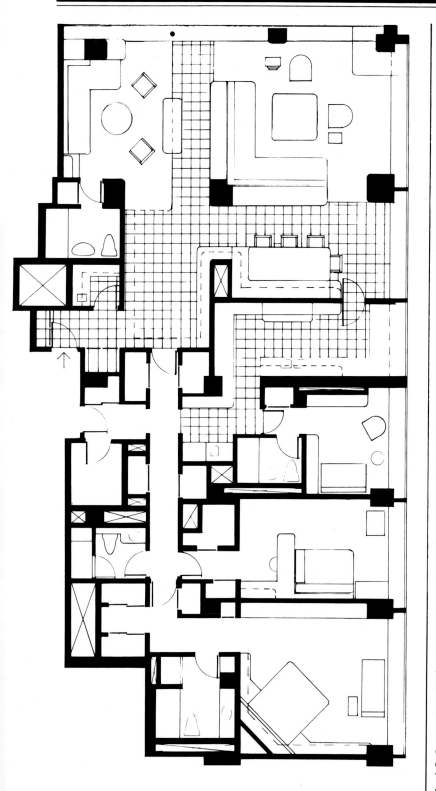

changes provide the needed textural diversity. In the living room, more formal fabrics are used—faille on the sofa, satin on the pillows, and suede on the chairs. The banquettes in the den and dining area are also leather covered, but here the opposite side of the hide is used.

There was some interesting thinking behind the art purchases, a collaborative effort between designers and clients. The obvious choice would have been to fill the ample wall spaces with large and preferably important works. But, Patino and Wolf made a conscious decision to avoid the obvious. "The greatest luxury these days is space," says Patino apropos the subject. "We wanted to make the space itself like a giant piece of sculpture; we didn't want or need to gild the lily." The works they purchased are, for the most part, small; they neither dominate a room nor demand the viewer's immediate attention. (The Nevelson, the only large piece, was existing.) They are not wall-affixed and can be moved at will—an idea that the designers favor. "Once you move a piece of art, it becomes new again. You see it differently." None of this, however, is to detract from the value of the works purchased. They include the Henry Moore sculpture that sits on a revolving base and is meant to be viewed from living and dining areas, a Picasso drawing, and an Irving Penn photograph. Also considered as works of art are the carefully edited accessories: silver candle sticks by Elsa Peretti, a 16th-century Chinese celadon plate, an Egyptian mask, and a collection of 17th-century Chinese porcelains displayed in a wall niche in the master bedroom. **E.C.**

OPPOSITE PAGE

Above: Although given definition as an individual function area, the dining room is still part of the overall living space. The custom table is of oak with steel detailing and seats eight to ten. The console opens on the dining side to reveal storage for table service.

Below: View of the den whose boundary is suggested by the free-standing partition storing audio/visual equipment. (The reverse side of this element frames the Nevelson work.) The custom table is also of oak with steel detailing, and can be raised from cocktail to dining heights.

Understanding Understatement

Left: View of the wife's study which doubles as a guest room. The desk was oriented to capitalize on the view.

Below: View of the husband's bathroom, fitted in the same oak used for table surfaces, and reminiscent of a bath found on a luxury liner.

Wall colors in the master bedroom are in varying shades of peach, with the wall behind the bed lacquered an apricot color. Behind the bed are niches for display of a collection of 17th century Chinese porcelains purchased by the designers. Other artworks include the Picasso drawing and a Nevelson box. The telephone panels are finished in polished brass and fitted into the end tables.

The commission had all the ingredients to fulfill any designer's fantasy: a huge duplex apartment on Manhattan's Sutton Place with views of the East River, a virtual sky's-the-limit budget, and a client whose close ties to the theater made him receptive to the most dramatic scheme that anyone could devise. So designer Mario LoCicero gave free reign to his imagination and came up with a solution that does indeed provide an initial impression of "drop-dead" glamour. Yet on closer examination, one discovers the intricacy and pervasiveness of the detailing. And it is, in fact, this aspect that isolates the apartment from others in its class.

Starting with an interview process to determine the direction that renovation would take, LoCicero learned that his client preferred a neutral palette and wanted the space to be "timely, yet have a quality of timelessness." Then, the designer recalls, "I asked where he had been in the world that most intrigued him." His response named not a specific place, but dealt with a past era. He spoke of a missing sense of quality and service, and then went on to talk of his fascination with

After entering the apartment on the upper level, one descends the stainless steel and brass stairway to the living room, a 40 x 28' space built to recall a suite on the Normandie. Furnishings are few; six small-scaled leather covered chairs and a chaise longue are divided into two groups, each around an identical lacquered cocktail table. The end wall, a custom storage unit for entertainment needs, is highlighted by two floor-to-ceiling columns of beveled glass that are lit from behind. The general contractor was Manfred Hecht. The music system was created by Peter McKeon.

Photographer: Jaime Ardiles-Arce

The Thirties Revisited

A Manhattan duplex by Mario LoCicero recalls
a suite on the Normandie

The Thirties Revisited

It was partially demolished to open the space. Behind the columns (which are just under ceiling height) and house uplights, making them resemble huge torchères, the elevation separating the main space from the kitchen and guest bath was rebuilt as a curved wall. The focal point of the entire apartment, however, is the stairway. This wave of stainless steel and brass, complete with Allen head screws for detailing, was installed to completely alter the angle of access to the living room from the main entry and balcony above. LoCicero interviewed six engineers before finding one to undertake the project, he recalls.

The furnishings are surprisingly simple. Mirrors throughout are bronzed. The same dark wool tweed carpeting covers all floors (except baths and kitchen) and the platform/headboard treatment in the master bedroom. The living room uses only six leather covered chairs (specially reduced in scale) and a chaise longue as seating elements. They are divided into two groups, each around an identical lacquered cocktail table. The dining table, a glass top on a lacquered pedestal, rests behind one of the columns. There are no permanent dining chairs; folding chairs are removed from storage when needed.

Clearly, this was a special project that provided the designer the luxury of creating a total installation. "There were even special budgets for accessories and kitchen cooking equipment," says LoCicero. It also provided the designer the opportunity to maximize a personal credo: "An environment should be more than the client expected it to be."   **E.C.**

luxury ocean liners and the Art Deco era. From there, LoCicero continued the association, introducing his client to the merits of Bauhaus design. In this roundabout manner, the design theme was set. The space would be rebuilt to recall a suite on the 1930's luxury liner—specifically the Normandie. Yet, the interpretation would be entirely figurative. For the solution would make use of modern technology to have the apartment function like a piece of precision-made machinery.

Two-and-a-half years in the works (but only three days in the conceptual stage), the project began with total restructuring of the interior. Alterations, too numerous to list in entirety, include the following: Throughout, the ceiling was lowered to accommodate recessed lighting. The area between the two aluminum-clad columns, themselves an addition, originally had been a solid wall.

Above left: The dining table—situated behind one of the aluminum-clad columns—is a simple glass top on a lacquered base; folding chairs are removed from storage when needed. The sculpture on the table is by Huguenot and comes from the Muriel Karasik Gallery.

Opposite: The bedroom, too, is mirrored with bronzed glass. The bed treatment is a mattress recessed into an undulating platform which is banded underneath with brass and then lit. Special cove lighting was installed behind the blinds, which here conceal views of the Queensboro Bridge. The closets have custom fittings inside.

Photographer: Dan Forer

Regional Resonance

*Overtones of the south-western style
stand out in a Florida residence
designed by Raymond W. Boorstein, ASID*

Initially the client's assignment called for the professional design of a family room only. Small and rectangular, the designated area—as held true for all main spaces in the Hollywood (Florida) tract house—was conventionally enclosed within full-height walls.

But Raymond Boorstein, the interior designer, considered the brief too confining. To do the job properly and take into account living needs, he suggested, the family room should not be divorced from the living space. The dividing partition, therefore, ought to be deleted.

Client response was tepid. Whereupon Boorstein sketched out the layout he envisioned, and in almost no time at all, skepticism changed to enthusiasm. Which extended not only to proposals for the one room but also to additional work encompassing the entire main level.

From then on, free rein in going ahead with architectural and interior design was the order of the day. Asking for one consideration only—that the feeling of the south-west, as expressed by some pottery pieces collected previously, be reflected internally—the clients endorsed Boorstein's plan to remove rigid partitions throughout and to create a large open space implicitly defined by angled soffits, partial walls, platforms, and down-lights. The recast layout now visually suggests diverse function areas consisting of a raised segment for small-group seating, separate dining area, foyer, and large living space for entertaining and leisure pursuits.

The requested south-west theme was implemented through

Platform-raised seating area, seen from foyer **(left)** and from rear of main living space **(below)**, holds four leather-covered barrel chairs and glass-top coffee table with plaster-composition tree trunk base. Rug-draped partition shields dining segment. After removal of full-height walls, the popcorn ceiling was refinished to its original texture and painted in a warm tan shade. Supplementary seating and display space are provided by two cushioned steps (horizontal view, right) and tiled structure (background), the latter doubling also as serving counter. Artworks include: orange/blue pastel picture by Lee Simpson from Ledoux Gallery, Taos; wall-hung plate by Georgia Sartous from Clay & Fibre, Taos; square white plate by Dintenfass from Hills Gallery, Santa Fe; and ceramic dish (on coffee table) by Nambé.

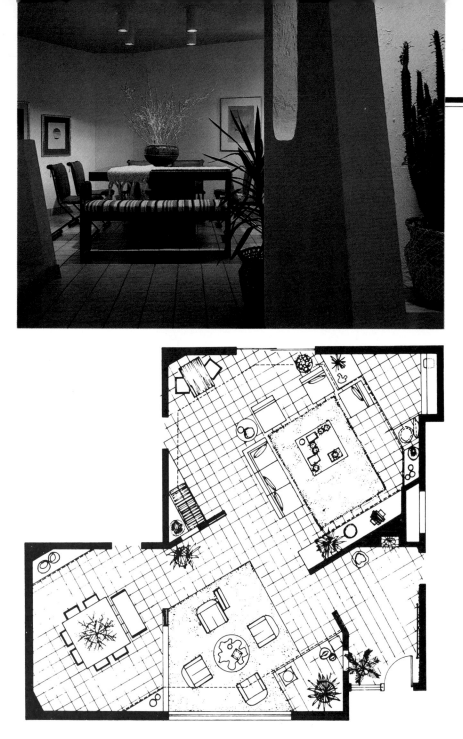

◄ **Dining area,** seen here from the center of the living room. In place of a conventional center piece, a hammock is draped across the extension top. Similarly avoiding the obvious touch is the use of plain rather than decorated tiles. Framed picture at left, by Don Jones, is through Santa Fe Artist Co-op; large bowl, by Henry Mead, through Panache of Denver.

architectural and decorative motifs such an angular forms, quadracurve see-through niches, adobe-like wall textures, natural materials, and the palette of the stipulated region. Additional artworks, selected with Boorstein's guidance even as work progressed, were bought by the clients and now are important components of the south-western scheme. With the exception of two brought-along pieces, furniture is newly bought or custom-built. Cabinetry throughout was done by a craftsman on the designer's staff.

In summing up, Boorstein's major preoccupation, it would seem, focuses more on expressing appreciation of the clients than claiming credit for himself. Not only did they make it a pleasure to do the job, he asserts, but also, their support and receptiveness-to-suggestions accounted for its success entirely. More objective endorsement comes from the Interior Design Guild of Florida which named Boorstein the 1982 Designer of the Year (first place, creativity in single space) in recognition of the house shown here.   **M.G.**

Another part of the living area focuses on a square coffee table in front of laminate cabinets accommodating stereo equipment, television and general storage. Out of the camera's range here but seen on the **cover** is a bar set on an elevated level. Mobile wind chimes are from the Valley Forge Gallery in Vail, Colo.; artists represented through pottery pieces on acrylic shelves are Stella Teller, Juanita Fragua, Lisieta, Presilla Namingha Nampeyo, and Rich Dillingham.

Regional Resonance

When Stephen Levine and Laverne Dagras (husband and wife in private life, collaborating architect and interior designer as professionals) moved into this post-war Manhattan cooperative, they did so fully cognizant of its plus and minus aspects. Listed as assets were size—a three-bedroom unit of approximately 1500 square feet, and an acceptable floor plan that separated living and sleeping quarters. On the minus side, says Levine, "there were entry problems, closet problems, and architectural detailing problems." So a fairly detailed architectural restructuring was in order even though the basic room configuration was left intact.

Entering the space in its "before" stage, Levine recalls, one had no sense of proper entrance. Instead of an anteroom, one was propelled directly into the living room. First the couple took out the extraneous closet to clear the space. Then, they created two painted screens—one of them free-standing, the other semi-attached—to suggest a foyer, and help to define the axis that carries one through the living room beyond (see plan).

The second problematic category—storage for the baths and master bedroom—was solved by gutting that rear corridor and creating back-to-back closets. Further, the entry to the bedroom was moved to create a dressing area (again refer to plan).

What Levine terms the "architectural detailing difficulties" were perhaps the most challenging to resolve. In the living room, a "lumpy" column—structural support and a chase for steam heat pipes—protruded into the room along the window wall. It was cut down, shaped, stepped and painted pale mauve, turning it into the kind of architectural detail most apartment dwellers crave. The stepped treatment, which has developed over the years into a Levine signature, is not, however, mere applied decoration. Instead, it represents a solution to a specific problem. The treatment is a transition element, bridging the gap between adjacent, yet uneven, planes. This detail is repeated for the same reason at the apartment's entry, and also in the newly curved wall enclosing the kitchen. Here, the formerly angular wall had to be pushed

Shaping Up

Stephen Levine and Laverne Dagras restructure their Manhattan co-op

Shaping Up

This page: One of the three bedrooms doubles as an office. The room is furnished with a pair of facing Murphy beds that can be concealed by a sliding wall. Photographs illustrate the room in both aspects. The rug is an antique from Tunisia.

Opposite: A sense of entry was established, first through the creation of two screens, second by the dropped soffit that accommodates incandescent lighting. The screens have marble ledges and built in cabinets facing the dining area, where ten prints of Alber's Variant series are displayed.

back and curved in order to accommodate the refrigerator and cabinets along a flush front. Additionally, a sliding door was added to this end wall, thereby providing access to the kitchen from either dining or lounging areas of the main space.

Although the sitting and dining divisions could have been in any configuration given the double-sided access to the kitchen, the windowed elevation with view west to Central Park dictated that the living area would be grouped nearby, while the dining table and chairs would be positioned near the entry. Furnishings themselves are modern classics. "They are clean looking, but comfortable and not stark," says Ms. Dagras, adding that each seating piece was selected for the way it sits. Materials—marble, leather, and wool—show a harmony of smooth textures set within the neutral background that allows the fine detailing of the space to stand out. The accent shades of deep raspberry and pale mauve display altering hues throughout the course of the day as the nature of the daylight changes.

Since an architect's or designer's own space often best describes his work, we asked Levine for comment on the subject. "Every job," he says, "has inherent problems that can be solved in either a standard or different way. Sometimes, there is a way of solving a problem with a solution that has inherent design value, that is more interesting. There's an undercurrent of orneriness to my work—a refusal to follow standard solutions." **E.C.**

New Directions

Kevin Walz explores new materials, shapes and colors in his design of a Manhattan apartment

What has happened to Kevin Walz? Known as a proponent of minimal (for want of a better term) design, he seems here to have joined forces with those who favor softer lines and an increased opulence of materials. Gone—at least in this case—are the white walls, built-in furniture, and everything associated with the industrial aesthetic. Yet, he maintains, the project is still based on the sensibilities to which he has always adhered: a preference for strong sculptural forms coupled with the experimentation of new materials.

So much for prologue. This is a three-bedroom flat in an Upper East Side (Manhattan) luxury high-rise. First off, says Walz, "there was a strong geometry about the place; the idea of symmetry became important because the apartment was full of it." Just one example —the long but relatively narrow main space encompassing the living room, dining room and entry (see plan). Structural changes, then, went to reinforcing the theme of symmetry. Corner columns were evened. The entry foyer, whose large size was inordinate to its amount of use, was transformed to act as a "transitional" pass-through between living and dining rooms. First, its scale was visually reduced by dropping the ceiling to a perforated stainless steel plane and by

painting the walls twilight blue. Then, he formed two facing curves to add both dimensional interest and suggest boundaries.

In the living room, he emphasized the strong lines of the corner columns by painting them matte charcoal. To continue this symmetry on a horizontal plane, he created ledges on both sides of the lengthwise elevation and covered them with a dark grey carpet that matched the column color. Building on this theme with his furniture configuration, the designer created two mirror-image groups at either end of the living room, with the more formal sofas near the window wall. Bridging the two groups is a third seating element formed by three floor and three back cushions. This in turn faces a central wall niche ("where a fireplace might have been") housing the large-screen television. All the seating (as is virtually all the furniture) are custom designs, and represent the designer's most comprehensive design of free-standing furniture pieces in a completed project.

The use of strong color marks a departure from the mostly monochromatic palettes of previous projects. Yet the harmony of black, blue, grey, pink and ecru tones ought to come as no surprise, given Walz's background as a fine arts painter. "These are urban colors,"

An oversized entry foyer was made into a pass-through between living and dining rooms. It was made more intimate by dropping the ceiling and painting walls a twilight blue shade.

Photographer: Peter Vitale

Above: The edge of the dining room is suggested through placement of a custom server, finished with a laminate of a grey base with copper fibers running through it to lend an opalescent quality. The black walnut table seats ten with Fledermaus chairs. The Chinese vase is the first antique Walz purchased for a client.

Opposite: The living room has two seating groups bridged by a large chaise that faces the recessed large-screen television. Uplights are incorporated into the two ledges that run lengthwise through the room. Supplementary lighting comes from floor lamps; there are no overhead fixtures.

New Directions

he says, and goes on to explain that they were selected by standing on the terrace with the clients and choosing those colors of the city reflected in the surrounding buildings. The tones here, he asserts, have none of the pastel quality associated with those of Postmodernism. The colors were right for the space and right for the clients. They were not selected due to current stylishness.

Along with the lush colors comes a correspondingly lush selection of materials—black stained oak for cabinetry, black walnut for the dining table, cotton velvet and linen for upholstery fabrics, and an unusually stitched iridescent silk textile for the master bedspread. "I'm interested in the visual as well as the textural qualities of materials," he says. "It's not decorative to work with these types of materials. To me, decoration is disguise and that's different from design."

There is no art in the dwelling, and this decision rested solely with the clients. "They wanted the walls to be like a taut skin; they wanted the space to be the thing."

Concluding with two sentences, Walz sums up the essence of the installation. "There's a sensibility about the space. It's part of the 20th century—of our era—yet it's not dated to any particular day." **E.C.**

Timeless Taste

A Manhattan apartment by Noel Jeffrey, ASID

Noel Jeffrey, ASID, designed this Upper East Side (Manhattan) cooperative more than four years ago. But, to anyone's eye, he might have completed it yesterday. For, it is based on Jeffrey's stated tenets of contemporary classicism—uncomplicated open spaces, simple furniture lines to let the materials take precedence, and clean backgrounds either to enhance the display of art or stand on their own. Yet as much as the project reflects Jeffrey's ideas, so too does it respect the client's tastes. For his input influenced both the space alterations and the selection of the color palette. Further, according to the designer, this is an interior meant to encourage the client to add objects of his choice. What is shown here, is by no means intended to remain unchanged over the years.

Starting with the physical confines, Jeffrey either ripped out or moved every wall but those enclosing the apartment. The result: a transformation from what had been a broken-up area with small closed-off rooms and long narrow corridors into a single spatial expanse. It starts at the now-proper entry and follows around a curved storage wall to an L-shaped living/dining area. Structural work also entailed "trying to improve the architecture by evening up the beams," says Jeffrey, and lowering the entry foyer ceiling to 7′10″.

For finishes and furnishing selections, the designer was, in effect, granted carte blanche. The client's loose directive was wanting "something cool and summery with the lightest possible colors juxtaposed against high gloss white walls so that decorative pieces would stand out." These pastel tones—lavender, pink and green—are currently much in vogue as part of the signature palette of post-Modern stylists. Yet, at the time they were selected for this project, "no one was using these colors," says Jeffrey. They are deployed as subtle accents—just enough to enliven the neutral scheme, yet not enough to date the apartment once the color pendulum shifts direction.

Opposite: A proper entry foyer was created from a series of small, chopped up spaces. The ceiling here was lowered to match the beam height of the living room. One wall was painted in a high gloss/matte stripe pattern to add interest to an area where there would be no art. The works on the opposite wall are three woodcuts by Gustave Baumann and an ink drawing by Rockwell Kent.

Photographer: Jaime Ardiles-Arce

146

The living room has been opened up to flow from the enlarged entrance and incorporates a dining area that formerly had been a closed-off room. The curved wall is a storage closet. The built-ins were custom designed for books, stereo equipment including exposed speakers, and for display of the client's antique glass. The sculpture behind the piano is an untitled work by Vasa, composed of pastel toned columns of fused glass. On the cocktail table are an oversized Victorian goblet and a pair of Indian heads by Haganauer. Dating back to the Deco era, one head is of bronze, the other of silver.

Timeless Taste

Timeless Taste

Furniture is based on classic forms, and although sparse in concentration, provides adequate seating and flexibility for entertainment purposes. Several items are of Jeffrey's design: the modular seating, the cocktail table and console with verde marble tops and lacquered bases, and the dining table with olive ash burl top on steel legs. Even the piano has been customized as an alternative to buying an old Deco piece. Jeffrey had the original legs and music stand removed, redesigned new ones, and had the piano lacquered taupe.

The art works in the apartment have been collected by the client over a period of years. He started by buying Western Americana works from the turn of the century, and then expanded his collection to include American works of the twenties and thirties. He also has an extensive collection of antique glass works in pastel or deep amethyst shades that show up beautifully against the glossy white backgrounds of the custom built-ins. **E.C.**

Above: The co-op's second bedroom was transformed into a den. Again, built-in cabinetry stores books, stereo equipment, and rare pieces of antique glass from Clichy Glassworks and St. Louis Glassworks. The painting is by Leatrice Rose; the vase is by John Copper.

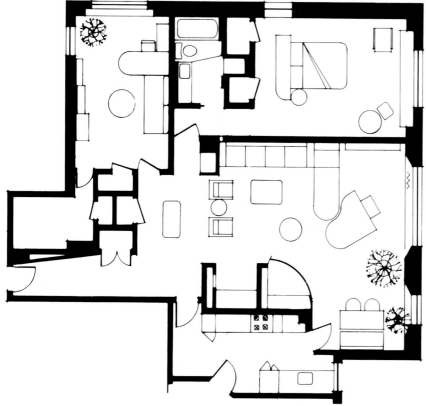

Opposite: For the master bedroom, Jeffrey created a lacquered headboard that not only provides storage/display space, but also partitions the room to designate an entry and dressing area. The striped bedspread fabric incorporates all the pastel shades of the client's preference. The drawings of nudes are by Maynard Dixon. The glass carafes and perfume bottles are also from the St. Louis and Clichy Glass Works.

Built-in Entertainment

*Anthony Machado creates
a luxury liner setting
for at-home diversions*

The commission for the interior design of the diamond as big as the Ritz would have been just Anthony Machado's cup of tea. This farm-bred young California designer revels in glamour, romance, and fantasy.

Our case in point is the entertainment suite that Tony Machado created out of the entire 1,200-square-foot top floor of a home in San Francisco's Pacific Heights. With windows on three sides (and a deck on the fourth) taking in spectacular bay views, the prospect might well be from A deck of a luxury liner. Without laboring the point, this is the illusion that the designer has effected. With its curves and strong color, built-in amenities and rich surfaces, the aura of the luxurious lounges of the late great ocean going liners is a strong subliminal suggestion throughout the suite.

The setting is an undivided sweep of space designed for a highly gregarious family with six children. The space includes a hobby area, a dining area, and two lounge areas perpendicular to one another, all unified by continuous carpeting and consistent materials, color, and detail.

Right: Built-in banquette and flanking storage units of the entertainment suite suggest the glamour of the great ocean liners, a look further suggested by the cartouche curves of the shelf and mirror elements. Brass-banded bleached oak storage unit opens to reveal a movie projector. The movie screen is contained in the slot of the ceiling beam. The designer's brass cylinder tables with inset onyx tops reiterate the columnar form of the lacquered cylinder containing television and stereo components. Beyond is a separate rear lounge area with painting by Dick Cohen.

Photographer: Jaime Ardiles-Arce

Built-in Entertainment

To create a calm order from the irregular fenestration on two walls of the gutted space Machado designed new perimeter walls of bleached oak with a regular rhythm of cartouche cutouts for the windows (see overleaf), and these curved elements are strategically reiterated—in the banquette wall of a lounge area, in the custom storage units of bleached oak, in a lacquered desk, in custom brass ceiling fixtures, even in the designer's double decker ottomans scattered about. The curves are completed in the cylinders of Machado's brass occasional tables and the bold brass-banded lacquered column that visually anchors a deep stretch of space while housing television and stereo components as well.

The brilliant matched lacquer surfaces of major elements are achieved with automobile paint—BMW lacquer finish, to be precise—which is even applied to the vertical blinds. Slick, reflective elements, as established by the gloss of the lacquer finish, appear in contrast to the matte finish of the cotton carpeting, suede cloth upholstery, and bleached oak components. These reflective elements—mirrored cartouches below the window cutouts, the mirrored wall behind the main lounge area, the ¾″ glass shelving in several locations, and the polished brass detailing—all serve to intensify, by day, the sparkling light quality of the bay setting.

After dark these reflective elements take on a different sort of sparkle, a festive glitter under the beams of low voltage ceiling fixtures—a special glamour for evening, which is Tony Machado's time of day.   **L.W.G.**

Above: Rear lounge area sums up the brass detailing throughout with its reflective ceiling, absorbing the sparkle from the bay. Double decker custom ottoman is one of several scattered throughout.

Opposite: The swoop of a custom fluorescent light fixture follows the curves of a lacquered desk. Across the room, beyond the dining table, a cartouche cutout perimeter wall of bleached oak masks irregular fenestration. Pedestal for the brass deer is a stereo speaker. Lucite candlesticks are Machado designs.

Chapter 5

Loft Apartments

Lofty Living

A Manhattan residence created by Kevin Walz in a 4000 square foot loft

This is a story about two personalities, client and designer with out-of-the-ordinary backgrounds, who worked together to create an extraordinary design project, The client Adri, a fashion designer who goes by her first name only, had lived in a conventional Upper East Side one-bedroom apartment. Opting for a radical change in her life, she purchased this 4000-square-foot loft located in the midst of a manufacturing sector, against the advice of all friends. She then asked Kevin Walz, who also lives in the building to design the space. But Walz was a fine arts painter by profession, not a trained designer. Until then, his sole interior project had been the loft/studio that he shares with his wife Barbara, an accomplished photographer. His design expertise and knowledge of things technical comes from a self-taught, four-month total immersion course.

Walz, however, had several assets because of his prior training. In a confident, yet low-keyed manner, he speaks of his awareness of the strength of individual forms and the spatial relationships among them. He also has developed a sensitivity to proportion and scale, and of course to the subtle nuances of color and light. "I have an intuitive grasp of three-dimensional space, and I love problem solving," he says. Lest one attribute this successful start to a stroke of beginner's luck, Walz has since completed nearly 30 interior projects, both residential and commercial.

Preliminary structural work was comparatively minimal. The loft has large expanses of windows on all four elevations, and the panes in every window needed replacing. Almost two-thirds of the original flooring was in acceptable condition; the remainder was replaced, and the entire floor was stained a silvery driftwood color and waxed. Walls were painted five different shades of white to play up the light that streams in and changes color according to the time of day. There were no walls installed since Adri did not want standard partitions to define areas.

The client did have fixed criteria. "First, she specified that this not be 'a woman's space.' She wanted it to be a neutral, architectural environment," Walz explains. Further, she requested that it be flexible and open, yet there were to be areas for particular functions. Thus, there are individual "islands" for lounge seating, dining, cooking and sleeping, each suggested by the furniture comprising it, not by fixed partitions. To the rear of the loft is an exercise station with rings, ballet bar and gym mat; in the center is a large Jacuzzi whirlpool tub. The client also wanted to rethink some of the conventional aspects of an apartment such as storage and lighting.

Above: The designer, seated at the client's baby grand piano with a view of Manhattan behind him.

Opposite: A carpeted platform resting on a mirrored recessed base for seating and a cocktail table are the only pieces of furniture in the living room. To the left of the piano is one of the several free-standing storage/lighting units found in the space. The back is open and fitted with shelves.

Photographer: Mark Ross

157

Lofty Living

The criteria set, Walz anchored his "islands," and designed furnishings for them. Furnishings are sparse in concentration and are based on strong clean lines. For the living area, seating is carpet-covered platforms that rest on a recessed mirrored base. These platforms, coupled with a Robsjohn-Gibbings-designed cocktail table and baby grand piano from her former residence, are the only furniture items. What appear to be large free-standing lighting fixtures are actually custom designed storage units. The fronts are solid except for the niche housing a fluorescent tube (over which colored gels are placed to create atmospheric changes); the backs are open and fitted with shelves to accommodate stereo equipment, records and books. These units, which appear again in the dressing area for clothing storage, are constructed of lacquered wood on a recessed mirrored base. They are mobile and easily moved to suggest alternative spatial divisions.

For the dining area, Walz and the client decided that four small square tables would suit her living and entertaining requirements more than a single large one

Above is a view looking from the entrance across the living area. To the rear is a storage unit with an orange gel over the fluorescent bulb. **Opposite** are views of the dining area with its four separate tables (top) and the sleeping and exercise areas (bottom). In the dining area view, the partition to the right separates it from the kitchen. Just beyond are steps up to the raised platform that surrounds the whirlpool bath. For the sleeping area, Walz built a platform for the king-sized bed, eliminating the need for any tables or additional furniture. Behind the head of the bed are two storage units for Adri's clothing.

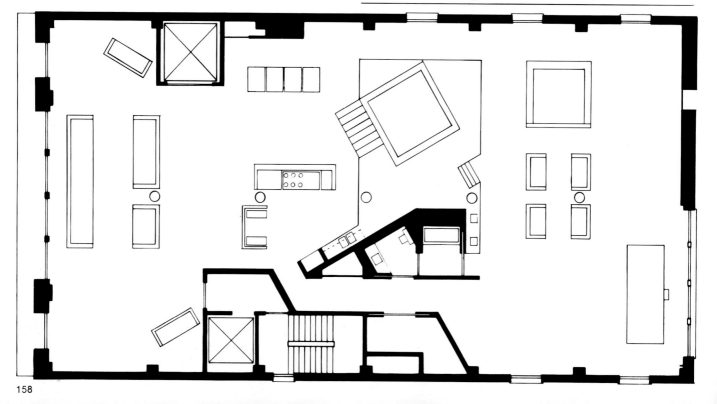

would. This gives Adri the option of entertaining both large and small groups of people. Separating the dining area from the kitchen is a 54"-high partition that gives the client her desired privacy when preparing food, but does not completely isolate her from guests.

The whirlpool bath is a luxury item requested by the client. To minimize its volume, Walz created a platform surround which makes the 36"-deep pool appear to be only one-third that depth. Pragmatically, the raised platform provides storage space for filtering equipment and it also serves to link the pool to other areas in the loft. On one side, the raised platform continues into the kitchen to become a work counter; on another side it becomes the vanity table surface in the dressing area.

When asked if he encountered any outstanding difficulties as a beginning designer, Walz responds in the negative. The installation progressed smoothly and was completed in less than five months. Adri's loft has helped to create a new life not only for its owner but also for its designer.   **E.C.**

Left: According to Walz, the best view comes from sitting in the center of the tub. Walz built the surrounding platform to minimize the scale, making the pool appear to be 12" instead of its actual 36" depth.

Below: View of the kitchen. The client wanted her pots, pans and cooking equipment out on display. The designer objected. A compromise was reached when he suggested that one of the free-standing storage units be used; this one is modified to have an open front. This way the equipment is out, yet given a sense of place.

Opposite: Rings, a ballet bar, exercise mat and mirrored wall create an at-home gym for the client. The contractor for the project was Bill Post.

Photographer: Ivan Gray

Imagine being a Manhattanite living in a fairly large (at least by New York standards) but dark Upper West Side apartment, and finding on the market 3500 square feet of loft space with huge windowed exposures facing north, south and east. Then imagine having a designer for a brother who could custom build (in every aspect) a residence and be willing to complete the project on a piecemeal basis over an extended time period.

This is the story of "clients" Murray and Gail Bruce, a commercial film maker and painter respectively, and designer Angus J. Bruce. Angus accepted the challenge not only for its obvious reasons, but also as an opportunity to use this as a testing ground for furniture which might later be modified and shown in his West Broadway gallery. It took three years for the totally raw space (without even plumbing or electrical lines) to reach its present state. Even now it is not completed. Funds, of course, are the main reason. Costs kept increasing. And says Bruce, "everything we did required such tremendous quantities of material." He originally estimated $30,000 as the sum required to make the place liveable, but plumbing alone came to half that figure.

After acquiring the space and dealing with the immediacies of plumbing, wiring, removing the dropped ceiling to allow for a 17-foot height, and putting down a sub-flooring, Bruce was faced with the volume itself. How to divide it? How to reduce it to a liveable scale without detracting from the luxury of wide-open space? His subsequent solution is an unqualified success that is immediately evident on personal inspection.

Since this was to accommodate working facilities for husband and wife, Bruce first partitioned off 2000 square

View of the entry. Behind the rounded column is the stair leading to the guest bedroom which is open to the rest of the space. Behind the shoji screens is daughter Dakota's room. The flooring is oak as is the wood trim throughout.

The Luxury of Space

Angus Bruce designs a 3500-square-foot loft

The Luxury of Space

feet for his brother's production company. About half of this is office space (pictured) complete with built-in projection equipment; the other half is an open space used for casting, studio work or any other aspects of the production process. The work space is completely closed off from the residence, and even has a separate entry from the elevator vestibule.

For the residential sector, "the object was to divide the volume without building walls that would block out the light," says Bruce, adding, "You can see the sun rise and set from here." Yet, there were to be specific areas, each carefully defined within the whole. The floor plan that evolved is one based on a change in levels including a partial second story. This not only defines each area, but also increases the amount of square footage for living space (by about 1000 square feet) and takes maximum advantage of the panorama. Thus, the "living room" is five steps up at one corner of the space, with Gail's studio sector opposite. The "sunken" space in between became the kitchen whose focal point is a custom work island encompassing stove, warming oven, drawer and cabinet storage, and an eating counter. The dining table (eventually to be replaced by one of Bruce's designs) is logically placed behind the kitchen. Bedrooms—both master and guest—are up a flight of stairs and become aeries open to the rest of the house. The master bedroom is over the painting studio; the guest room with its own small bath is above the entry. Should the clients wish, they can render the bedrooms private spaces with the addition of shoji screens or perhaps glass doors. But, to date, they have no such plans. The only conventional "room" (except for the baths) is located to the left of the entry and is closed off with shoji screens. It was originally planned as a library, but with the arrival of daughter Dakota, it was transformed into a nursery.

Actual furnishings are few in number, and virtually all are designed by Bruce. "I was able to give them *exactly* what they wanted. For example everything is the

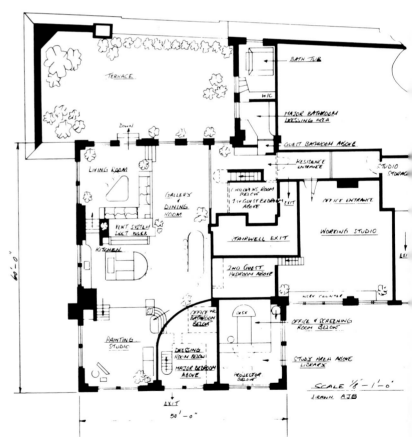

OPPOSITE PAGE

Gail's painting studio is a raised area in one corner of the loft. The rounded structure houses the upstairs master bedroom which, like the guest room, is open to the space below. Doorways, such as this one, are arched because Bruce is partial to curvilinear forms.

THIS PAGE

Views from the studio into the "sunken" kitchen. The island, of Formica with butcher block top, meets cooking, storage and eating needs.

The Luxury of Space

right height. If we didn't like something, we changed it."
Multi-function is a key word in the Bruce vocabulary,
and one sees it immediately in his design of the kitchen
pieces, the production room work table and the stereo
console. Less obvious are his design of the marble
topped coffee table with concealed ottomans on casters
and the banquette seating unit with built-in storage ca-
pacity. In fact, Bruce was so concerned with function
that he cut "trap doors" into the floors of the painting
studio and living room so that the below-level space
could be used for storage.

This then is a project that evolved out of a very special "partnership" between client and designer. It could
not have been done otherwise.   **E.C.**

Chapter 6

Designed for collections of art and antiques

Photographer: Mark Ross

Think of a room filled with fine antiques. Too often, one conjures up an image of a formal space filled with furniture—little or none of it comfortable for seating. This was basically the situation encountered by Robert Lewis when introduced to this large Fifth Avenue apartment.

The clients had been living in the space for some 14 years prior to the building's cooperative conversion. It was only after they had purchased the apartment that they decided on professional design assistance. Their parameters were few but definite. They wanted to retain their traditional decor as much as possible within the existing structure, and they would not settle for any expensive and extensive remodeling. The job then, as Lewis tells it, was mainly one of selecting new backgrounds, planning a lighting program, designing upholstered seating for comfort and editing the clients' collection of fine antique furnishings that had been amassed over the years. **E.C.**

In the living room, Lewis edited the clients' collection of antique furniture and added upholstered pieces for comfortable seating. The color for the mottled glazed walls was chosen to complement the terra cotta head that sits on a French bronze and malachite table and the Chinese silk upholstery and pillow fabrics.

Traditional
on Fifth Avenue

*Robert Lewis bases his design of a cooperative apartment
on the clients' collection of fine antiques*

Traditional on Fifth Avenue

The dining room is furnished with the clients' existing pieces. The chairs are Hepplewhite designs with leather seats; the table and console are also English antiques. The flowers sit in eighteenth century Wedgwood Atlas potpourri jars borrowed from La Ganke Antiques. The watercolors are by Dali.

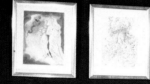

The Real Thing

*Authentic antiques and choice art prevail in a Park Avenue apartment
designed by Robert Martin, ASID*

After living in Westchester County for many years, the clients—a couple whose grown sons work in New York—decided to establish a second residence in a co-op apartment on Manhattan's Park Avenue. Their objective was to enjoy proximity to the husband's law office and the wife's cultural interests, while being able to entertain their family, business acquaintances, and friends. The mise en scène they envisioned was to offer contemporary comforts softened, however, with traditional warmth.

Robert D. Martin, their interior designer, spent nearly two years readying the new premises. Structural alterations involved conversion of two bedrooms and two bathrooms into one large master suite; absorption of a pantry into an enlarged kitchen; replacement of mouldings in the entrance hall, living and dining rooms; aligning of door heights and archways; and widening of the chimney breast. While this work was in progress the designer, after preliminary scouting of appropriate sources, took the wife to the showrooms for collaborative shopping. And at this point, as he tells it, a fresh dimension was added to the master plan.

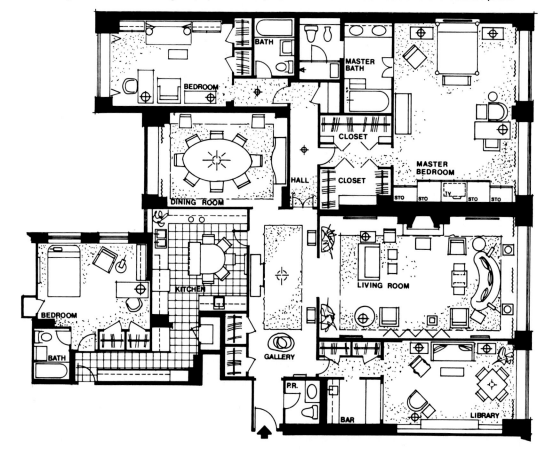

Waterford chandelier and Zuber wall ▶ covering made from original "Decor Chinois" wood blocks provide elegance in the dining room. Chairs were brought along from the clients' previous residence.

Photographer: Elliot Fine

First artworks visible upon entering the apartment are the imposing sculpture by Henry Moore and "Pisa North Station" painting by Daniel Lang.

In the living room, the proportions of the chimney breast were changed and mirror surfacing was added. (The reflected painting, partially visible, is by George Inness, 1825-94.) Martin refers to this and the other major spaces as being "formal, but neither stiff nor intimidating."

The Real Thing

The Past is Present

Richard Fitzgerald revivifies an 1830's townhouse to blend old-time grace with contemporary comforts

In what interior designer Richard Fitzgerald calls one of the largest and always-privately-owned townhouses on Boston's Louisburg Square, "former elegance has been restored while keeping in mind how people live in the 20th century." Other design objectives cited by Fitzgerald are "retaining the flavor of old Boston" by integrating into the interiors such furnishings as those used by the original inhabitants (the house was built in 1835, by Phineas Upham), while assuring present-day standards of comfort through the addition of new seating. The residence, over the years occupied by some of the country's most famous-name families, today houses a couple and one of their three children recently moved to town from the suburbs.

Except for the kitchen and garden deck, no architectural work was required to update the five-level structure. Backgrounds and all-new upholstery fabrics in the main living areas are kept subdued in shades of neutral beiges so as not to upstage the Georgian paneling of mahogany; subtle relief is supplied by the sparkle of crystal chandeliers. Typical of decorative touches is the copy of a large 18th century China Trade paper (behind the piano) which might have been in the possession of a Beacon Hill resident in the last century. Much of the furniture—mainly "English antiques with an American flavor"—was brought along by the owners. Supplementary seating pieces, lighting fixtures, carpeting and fabrics were selected by Fitzgerald with an eye to melding the compatibility of old and new appointments.

Obviously intrigued by the unique character of the building, Fitzgerald tends to underplay the account of his design work and draw attention instead to the rare qualities of the Greek

Formerly dark and visually confining, the hallway now appears lighter through the addition of mirrors at the end wall (where an elevator has been installed), under the stairway, and above the custom console tables. The latter are sliced halves of a tôle design with drilled-in holes to serve as air vents for radiators beneath. Walls are painted and glazed; architraves, mouldings, base boards and stair trim are marbleized "to give character" to the area. The paintings are by Charles Tausch.

Photographer: Jaime Ardiles-Arce

The Past is Present

The drawing room, located on the piano nobile, appears to consist of three separate segments: the "formal" area **(above)** at the front of the house, the fireplace-centered space **(opposite page)** in the rear, and the "lounge" in the middle.

The Past is Present

Revival-style dwelling and its surroundings: there is a public garden on the square in front, a private garden—landscaped by Stanley Underhill—in the rear; deft fitting and balance distinguish the granite stoop leading to the Doric portico; the entrance floor is elevated to create a basement area with full windows and service access; spacious dimensions—44′ 6″ by 17′ 6″—enhance the tripartite drawing room on the piano nobile (i.e., the main floor of the house containing reception areas); and finally there is the special ambiance of Louisburg Square which, particularly at Christmas time, becomes a communal enclave for householders from the vicinity. A. McVoy McIntyre, author of *Beacon Hill, A Walking Tour,* calls Louisburg Square "the gemstone . . . worn on Boston's cityscape."

M.G.

THIS PAGE:

Library/study, adjacent to the master bedroom.

Girl's bedroom, on the third floor.

Master bedroom on the second floor has glazed wall woodworking and linen toile-covered walls.

OPPOSITE PAGE:

The conservatory, attached to the dwelling structure, is used throughout the year as a greenhouse (the owner is described as a plant freak who himself takes care of the botanical chores) and serving center for informal refreshments.

Manhattan Duplex

When Luis A. Rey, of the venerable firm Mc-Millen, Inc., approached the redesign of this Manhattan duplex, his principal objectives were to open up the spaces and to arrange for the display of the clients' existing art collection (including the works of such artists as Picasso, Marisol, Gottlieb, de Kooning, Rauschenberg, and Dubuffet—among others) to best advantage.

The first floor of the 1600-square-foot apartment was originally divided into a separate entrance hall, dining room, and living room; the second floor consisted of two bedrooms and two baths. In the redesign, the only elements which were left relatively intact were the kitchen, the baths, and the stairwell; the remainder of the space was completely gutted although some existing marble paving was salvaged and reinstalled in a new angular configuration.

The revised first floor is essentially one flowing space (see floor plan) arranged on an angle—to the actual shell of the space—of 45 degrees. The diagonal configuration was chosen for two reasons: it made a somewhat run-of-the-mill space

The lower level was laid out on the diagonal to create a more interesting space and also create more planes on which to hang paintings. Trapezoidal coffee tables can be clustered in various configurations; mirrored ceiling well increases apparent ceiling height and reinforces the 45-degree axis of the space.

Photographer: Ashod Kassabian

*Art is the keynote in
an apartment designed
by Luis A. Rey of McMillen, Inc.*

more visually interesting and it also increased the number of wall planes on which the clients' large canvasses could be hung individually without any sense of "overlapping." Furniture was kept to a minimum: three built-in, carpet covered platforms incorporating banquette seating surround the perimeter of the space. Six custom-designed coffee tables, on casters and trapezoidal in plan, can be easily moved about to be used alone or clustered to form a variety of larger table sizes in differing shapes. The Mies MR chairs (two with arms and in wicker; four side models in leather) are lightweight and can be repositioned at will so that the room can be comfortably used to entertain as few as six to as many as twenty. The already low ceiling was lowered further around the perimeter of the space in order to accommodate recessed fixtures to light the artwork; however, by mirroring—again on a 45-degree angle—the two ceiling wells which resulted, the apparent ceiling height is dramatically increased and the diagonal orientation of the space is reinforced.

On the upper level, what had been two totally separate bedrooms were effectively fused by cutting through the intervening wall at two points and installing sliding doors (see floor plan). In general practice, these doors are left open to create one unified space—half of which serves as a bedroom and half as a study. However, to accommodate occasional guests, the doors can be closed so that the study becomes a second bedroom. The ceiling treatment on the upper level is similar to that below—in that the perimeters are dropped to house lighting—but in this case the wells are painted dark gray instead of mirrored.

Since showcasing the artwork was of primary importance, the color scheme for the installation is relatively neutral throughout. Virtually all the walls are painted gloss white; the carpeting, upholstery suedes and leathers, lacquered coffee tables, and floor tile and marble, are all in hues from the mid-brown range—with the single accent color being the bright red lacquer of the upper level's sliding doors.

The general contractor for the installation was William Crawford. **F.K.**

Above: Hall on upper level is dominated by a wall-mounted sculpture by Hinman; head on acrylic pedestal is by Marisol. The entrance to the bedroom area is to the left, directly ahead.

Opposite page: Formerly consisting of two separate bedrooms, the upper level now functions as a single unit with a bedroom area and study area. The study, however, can be used as a guest bedroom when the sliding doors are drawn.

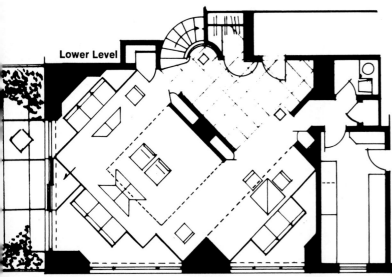

Lower Level

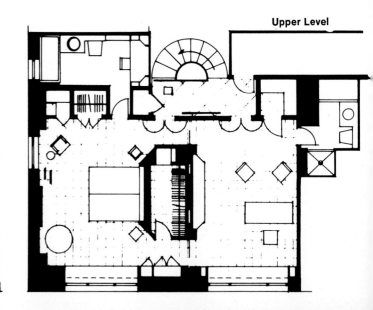

Upper Level

A Built-in Background

*Architectural forms and luxury materials complement the artwork
in a Manhattan co-op by Tom Foerderer*

Tom Foerderer's design of this Upper East Side (Manhattan) co-op shows his continued fascination with complex forms. Yet, this project differs distinctly from its predecessors. For here Foerderer was able to expand on his aesthetic with the introduction of luxury materials. His resulting statement, still architectural in character, is one of softened severity.

The apartment, his most elaborate project to date, underwent substantial structural alteration. All that remains of the original configuration are the centrally located mechanical core and the perimetrical/structural walls. Otherwise, all interior partitioning was demolished and the entire floor plan was redrawn. Now, there is a U-shaped circulation pattern, where visitors enter, progress through a long gallery with built-in dining banquette, and proceed to a rather small and inti-

Above: View of the entry with its built-in storage closet, mirrored coat closet, and another mirrored door leading to the guest wing. The long view through the gallery to the terrace is punctuated by a series of curved forms.

Opposite: A storage cabinet with recessed display case helps to differentiate the gallery from the living room (see drawing). All the figures were part of the clients' collection.

Photographer: Mark Ross

A Built-in Background

mate living room that actually doubles in function as a sitting room for the master suite beyond (see drawing). The opposite arm of the U, also directly accessible from the entry, accommodates a bedroom/den for the couple's grown children. Although each area is definitely delineated—primarily through changes in floor level with additional emphasis coming from new soffits and built-in furniture forms—the overall sense is of being in an open, almost loft-like space. Throughout, doors now slide into pocket enclosures, are mirrored on both faces, and are rarely closed.

Furnishings were designed and finishes were selected first, to complement the clients' art collection, consisting primarily of a superb collection of turn-of-the-century French posters amassed over the years. In fact, the artworks, coupled with the baby grand piano,

Above and opposite: Foerderer decided to locate the dining area in the long space used as a gallery. Since this area was the focal point of the apartment, clients and their guests could sit at the circular table (conducive to conversation) and enjoy cocktails or meals while seeing the posters. The seating banquette, whose form is mirrored by the ceiling treatment, incorporates storage space behind the black laminate doors. The custom table has a travertine top.

are the only pieces brought along from their previous suburban residence. Secondly, furniture was created to incorporate storage space, since virtually no wall space would be free for conventional solutions. A single color palette, based on variations of a beige/grey shade, runs throughout the apartment, and is implemented with the repetition of few materials. Walls and furniture forms are finished with semi-gloss lacquer; flooring materials are silver travertine or Berber wool carpet; channel-quilted raw silk covers the gallery wall, bed, and head wall. Contrasting with the pale tones is the cabinetry, all of which is finished with high-gloss black Formica and detailed with aluminum strips.

The lighting system is designed on highly controllable circuitry, and incorporates both recessed elements and special museum track fixtures with ultraviolet filters to spotlight art.   **E.C.**

Above: The master bathroom was rebuilt using the same travertine marble used in the entry. A large stall shower was installed to replace the tub, and there are separate vanities for the couple.

Below and opposite: The master bedroom is really a continuation of the "public" areas since it is colored in the same neutrals and uses the same wool carpet, raw silk, and cabinetry.

Chapter 7

The drama of black and dark backgrounds

Master of All Trades

Billy W. Francis handles all facets of design for a condominium apartment in Houston

In terms of basic needs and personal likes, the client, a foreign businessman now living in Houston, knew exactly what he wanted. His apartment was to contain one area large enough to entertain up to 250 people. Dining facilities were to accommodate 20 guests for sit-down meals. His favorite colors—blue, purple and off-white—were to be used. Audio-visual electronic equipment was to be of the most advanced technology and highest calibre. And everything was to be all new and contemporary.

But when it came to functional execution and aesthetic interpretation of these desiderata, all decisions were left to the discretion of interior designer Billy W. Francis entirely. Meeting with the client (thereafter represented by his business manager) just twice, Francis (engaged on the strength of his reputation) assumed responsibility for every phase of the job: In collaboration with his staff architect Michael Ewin he acted as his own contractor, and took charge of construction, plumbing, electrical work, architectural drawings, space planning, and other aspects of total design.

To start, he gutted and restructured the two condominium units which had been conjoined into one 5900-square-foot apartment. Then he allocated about 3500 square feet for the living/entertaining area which parallels the contours of the building exterior to form a semi-hexagon shape. The room appears sunken in relation to the dining segment, the latter having been elevated to allow for rerouting of wires and pipes leading to the kitchen.

Above: Entry foyer with free-standing screen sheltering dining room at left, and view to studio straight ahead. Two flower paintings are by Lowell Nesbitt; the steel sculpture on pedestal is by Kenneth Snelson.

Opposite: Two of three separate seating groups in 3500-square-foot living area furnished with custom lounge-furniture, carpeting, and occasional pieces of stainless steel-with-glass or cremo marble. Artworks include painting commissioned from David Ligare, bronze sculpture (on marble cube) by Michael Steiner, and glass forms by Howard Ben-tre and Dale Chihuly.

Two more views of living area focusing on glass cabinet, finished with 27 coats of lacquer over silver leafing and housing archeological arts collection, **this page;** and third of three seating segments plus mirror reflection of dining room under vaulted marble-clad ceiling, **opposite.**

Master of All Trades

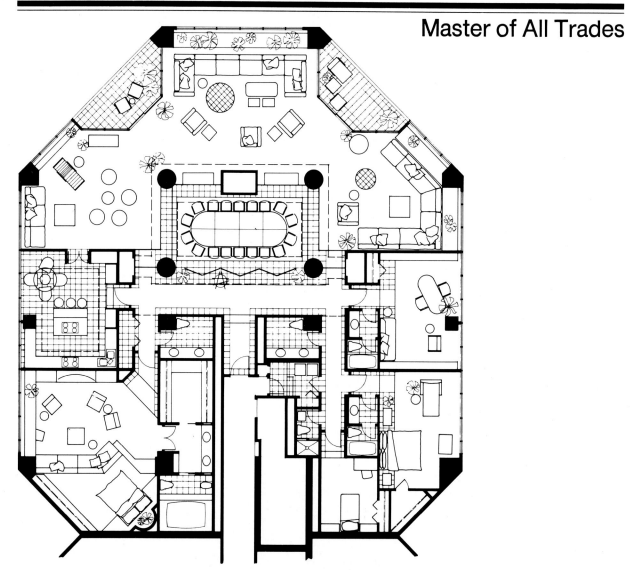

Kitchen, brought forward to windowed perimeter wall, now shares exposure to Houston skyline view. Cabinets and counters were designed by Jim Lockhart of Poggenpohl.

In dining pavilion, Italian cremo marble surfaces the vaulted ceiling, table top, cabinet and flooring. Stainless steel-and-etched-glass screen, seen from foyer side on previous page, forms backdrop at right. The entire room was raised from its original level to permit rerouting of plumbing and wiring.

Structural work included design of a free-standing screen, made of stainless steel with sand-blasted glass, which acts as divider between dining room and foyer. Similarly providing architectural interest is the vaulted dining room ceiling paved with 2"-square marble tiles. Still more innovative treatment pertains to finishes: 27 layers of lacquer over silver-leaf on built-ins, and blue lacquer baked onto glass in the bedroom/lounge area.

The stipulated color scheme provides a common denominator but is treated variedly to give identity to each room. Ceilings are triple-sprayed to produce a lavender/silver cloud effect, and walls are upholstered with fabrics in the palette's key tones. Italian cremo marble surfaces floors, dining ceiling, and casegoods. Carpeting, too, is custom designed.

The multi-media system, selected and built-in under Francis's direction, consists of hi-fi music components, ten television sets, Betamax, and projection equipment. All elements, including also light dimmers and draperies, are operable from master control panels located in the living space and bedroom/lounge.

In keeping with the "all new" specification, artworks also were bought or commissioned expressly for this residence. The entire project, in fact, covered all ingredients, right down to towels and linens and Tiffany silver, of a household custom planned for move-in readiness. Thus Francis, without undue exaggeration, indeed may claim—as he does—that the client took possession bringing little more than his toothbrush. **M.G.**

Cremo marble and iridescent lacquer millwork reappear in the ▶ study. Painting is by Bill Shepherd.

Elevated sleeping platform overlooks lounge area containing multi-media entertainment system controlled from cabinet left of bed. Walls are of deep blue lacquer on glass. Mirror reflection shows etched glass/steel doors leading to bathroom and dressing area.

Master of All Trades

Sophisticated Drama

*Juan Montoya's design of
an apartment in a
1910 Manhattan building*

The clients, Juan Montoya relates, wanted their Manhattan apartment to serve pre-specified needs. Additionally they asked for orderly cohesion, also a "sense of sophistication" and "feeling of enchantment" to make home-coming pleasant. "But the word that kept coming up most frequently," the designer recalls, "was *drama*."

And drama is what he gave them. Its impact becomes apparent immediately in the gallery-like foyer where shafts of light seem to lift the pedestal-supported art objects from the enveloping darkness. Then comes the living/dining area, integrated into a continuous flow of black-grey-white pierced by a massive red column. And everywhere there is point-counterpoint interplay of reflective and soft textures, ranging from mirrors and metals to tweeds and vinyl.

The largest area, previously divided into distinct living and dining segments by a squared mural-decorated column, now is treated as a single entity. Since a separate dining room was not needed, this section merely was raised and underlined with lighting, then framed with banquettes and a storage wall which, slightly angled, also conceals structural deformities. Used primarily for buffet spreads, the dining table—more sculpture than furniture—is anchored to the architectural upright.

It is this vertical element which serves as pièce de resistance and interior pace-setter. Built out with plywood and padded with Dacron fiberfill, it has been transformed from angular support beam into a rounded 30"-diameter column and given a sleek yet spongy surfacing of tautly stretched vinyl. Two lengths of 54"-wide material were needed and, to overcome the problem of seaming, were slotted into vertical black channels at mid-points. The curved shapes are repeated at the foyer junctions where, after removal of a door, somewhat smaller pillars were reshaped into ovals and wrapped with vinyl, black in this instance. Stereo equipment and bar occupy newly created space between the window and angled-out wall. Slanting of the now-mirrored wall extension, according to Montoya, produces the illusion of enlarged dimensions.

Foyer and off-shoot extension (above) create the effect of an artfully lit gallery, additionally setting the tone and tenor for the rooms beyond. Lighting, shining through cut-outs in lowered ceiling, focuses on 17th century Chinese white vase, 1920 Indian bronze, Art Deco vase, and 18th century Indian fabric painting. Slate flooring and lacquered surfaces (including old doors from the 1910 building) establish black framework. Only the mirrors are greyed.

Photographer: Jaime Ardiles-Arce

Formerly treated as separate entities, the living and dining areas now are unified into one cohesive space. Structural column in raised and under-lit segment has been built-out, rounded, and wrapped with padded vinyl; window wall at left was brought forward and angled to accommodate bar and stereo equipment. Plexiglas-encased 17th century Chinese scroll on pedestal, seen in **close-up,** acts as a barrier between mirrored backdrop and seating group to eliminate distracting image reflections. Ashanti stool is from the occupants' collection.

Sophisticated Drama

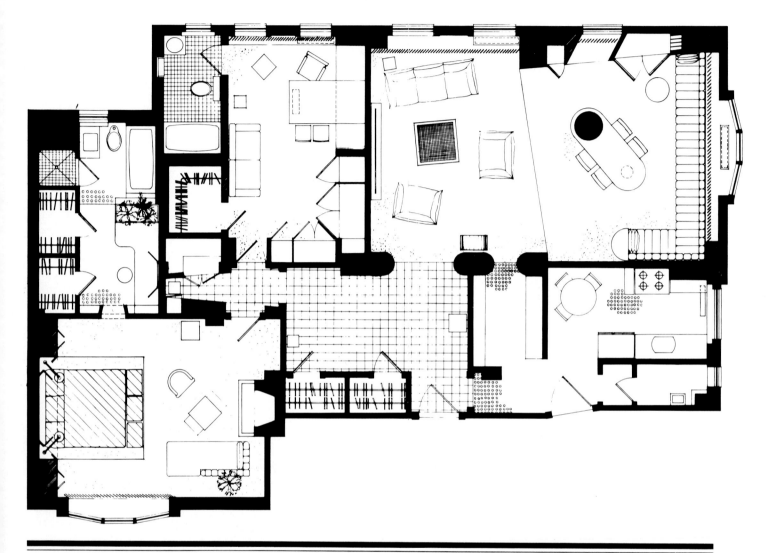

Sophisticated Drama

Mirrors, like the continuous carpeting and repeated round shapes, are among unifying elements. But their reflective qualities, while adding sparkle and appearing to magnify space, can prove distracting to people. Montoya, therefore, placed a pedestal upholding a Japanese scroll-under-Plexiglas between the mirror wall and lounge group. A dramatic display piece in its own right, the five-foot-high unit now acts as barrier shielding seated guests from image play-backs.

The entry segment sums up the tone and pace for the entire apartment. Additionally it bears evidence of Montoya's contention that architectural detailing, unless useless or ungainly, should be respected. Overhead beams devoid of character and grace were covered with a false ceiling which, in turn, hold lights recessed into cut-outs. But old doors were kept and, here as elsewhere, 1910-vintage mouldings were left visible. Lacquer paints and slate flooring form an all-black envelope lightened by greved mirrors.

M.G.

View from
Fifth Avenue

*Marcel Bretos creates a dark shell
to capitalize on city vistas*

High in a tower at One Fifth Avenue, this sleek apartment was designed by Marcel Bretos for a client who was leaving a too-large formal Central Park West residence in favor of a smaller space that could be transformed into the quintessential contemporary New York apartment. But like all too many Manhattan facilities, this small one-bedroom cooperative required extensive rebuilding to reach its pictured state.

After gutting the interiors, Bretos took the prow-like terminus of the living room as the basis for his design concept. Since there are four exposures here, and since this was to be "a real New York apartment," he explains, "we decided that there would be nothing better than to emphasize the windows and the view." He achieved this through two means. First, he created an all-black shell which allows the eye to move to the lightest area, i.e. the city panorama. Second, he used carefully placed mirrors including a unique band (placed at eye level when seated) that moves from the entry through the entire living room and dining sector. This creates what

Living room (18′ x 22′) takes maximum advantage of four windowed exposures through its dark background and use of mirror, including a band (at eye level when seated) that circles the room. The angled walls between the windows were constructed to imbue a sense of rhythm; elsewhere they were created to make the space more functional. The ceiling grid of stainless steel cable and turnbuckles conceals unsightly beams.

Photographer: Jaime Ardiles-Arce

View from Fifth Avenue

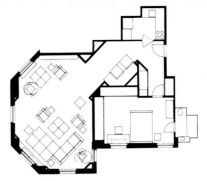

Bretos calls "a kaleidoscopic effect" by destroying the room's boundaries and multiplying the perspectives.

Mirror, plus the angling of walls, was also used to overcome the drawbacks of a small space and awkward circulation pattern. The entry, formerly just a long corridor, was widened and one wall was mirrored to reflect the living room and city beyond. From this "found" space, Bretos created a dining alcove with the addition of an angled wall. Directly opposite, he constructed another angled wall to form a bar area. Thus, the space is not only more functional, but also has a sense of movement that it would otherwise lack.

Two additional elements contributing to the overall drama are the ceiling treatment and lighting plan. The ceiling is an angled 15"-square grid of stainless steel cable and turnbuckles. Its solution was devised to detract from an unsightly confusion of beams. Lighting is based on specific shafts coming from spotlight fixtures; there is no true overall illumination. However, Bretos was careful to include floor lamps, making reading possible.

At first, this apartment may read as another of the all-black interiors enjoying current popularity. However, this, thanks to detailing, has a sense of movement, life, and even of light that others may lack.

Electrical work was by Falcone Electric Company; the lighting consultant was Frank Monteagudo.   **E.C.**

Above, left: Dining alcove was created when the entry foyer was widened and an angled wall constructed. The mirrored band reflects the bar that is opposite.

Below, left: The bedroom, although closed off, is essentially a continuation of the living room since the same elements are used in both. The painting is by Angel Romano.

Chapter 8

Designers Design for Themselves

Designer as Client

The Manhattan apartment by and for Adam Tihany

"Are you kidding?" So responds designer Adam Tihany to the obvious query: Is your apartment designed as a tour de force showcase for your work? "My house is for me and for my friends. I rarely take clients there."

The apartment, an at-ease-putting space housed in a pre-war building on Manhattan's East Side, makes no attempt to establish an identifiable style. Rather, it reflects Tihany's *approach* to residential design. (He does commercial work as well.) "To design a residence is a very personal thing; you design for a client, not for yourself. Every apartment I design is different. There is no common denominator; there is no identifying stamp. The only thing that you can teach a client is better use of the space. How that space will look decor-wise is completely subjective. What is aesthetically pleasing for a client may sometimes go against my taste. I have to get the client to participate. If there is no client dialogue, I might as well be designing a furniture showroom."

Tihany's apartment makes a very personal statement about his interests and those of companion Carol Lyon. He is an avid traveler and collector, accumulating objects wherever he goes. Thus, horizontal surfaces become display stands for his collections of miniature figures, antique architectural measuring instruments, antique brass accessories and humidors. More serious are the collections: of antique Venetian glass, which refers to his attachment to that city as well as the fact that he has designed glassware for some of the leading Italian manufacturers; of contemporary art by both proven masters (Claes Oldenburg, Robert Indiana,

Opposite views of the entry foyer with its mirrored columns which multiply the painting by Alberto Magnani and reflections of objects from the adjacent living room.

Photographer: Mark Ross

211

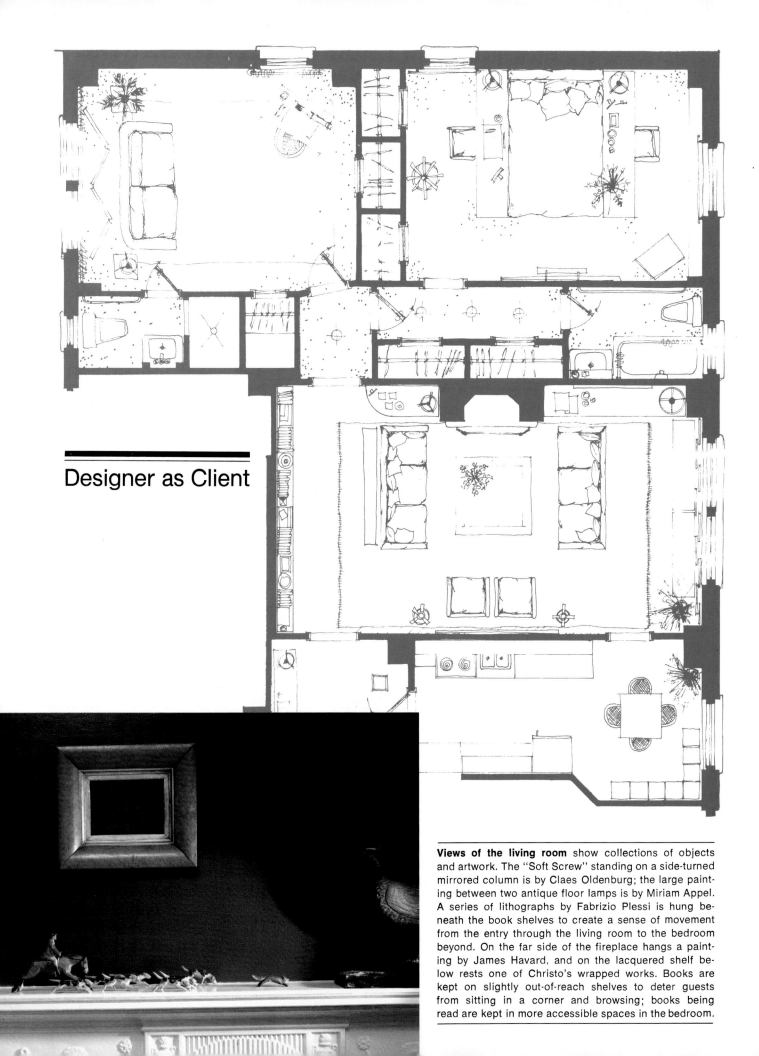

Designer as Client

Views of the living room show collections of objects and artwork. The "Soft Screw" standing on a side-turned mirrored column is by Claes Oldenburg; the large painting between two antique floor lamps is by Miriam Appel. A series of lithographs by Fabrizio Plessi is hung beneath the book shelves to create a sense of movement from the entry through the living room to the bedroom beyond. On the far side of the fireplace hangs a painting by James Havard, and on the lacquered shelf below rests one of Christo's wrapped works. Books are kept on slightly out-of-reach shelves to deter guests from sitting in a corner and browsing; books being read are kept in more accessible spaces in the bedroom.

Designer as Client

Above: In the living room, the fireplace mantel becomes a display stand for a miniature hunt collection. Note the painting-less frame—a bit of fun by Tihany.

Opposite, above: View of the bedroom where the blue and white color palette has been reversed. Lacquered desks with built-in shelving frame the two sides of the bed over which is a drawing by Saul Steinberg. The two works on the opposite wall are by Plessi.

Opposite, below: A lacquered shelf frames either side of the fireplace. One displays Ms. Lyon's collection of miniature dogs and Tihany's antique Venetian glass bottles. On the other are figurines of a Mexican orchestra and a wrapped work by Christo. Architectural measuring implements, which Tihany does use, rest on a custom storage console.

James Havard and Christo) and upcoming novices; and of antique furnishings such as the chaise longue, pair of floor lamps and rug.

Design is based on surface decor. No structural changes were effected since the apartment is a rental unit. The blue and white background —a change from the previous all-grey palette— was chosen, says the designer, because it is tranquil and "I think that it has something to do with my Mediterranean background." (He is a native Israeli who received his architectural/design training in Milan and worked there for several years.) He used a series of mobile mirrored columns to suggest architectural elements in the entry foyer and also to reflect images from the living room beyond. Furniture in the living room is placed not only to facilitate conversational groupings but also to suggest a traffic flow pattern.

All of the furniture is custom, and Tihany makes special mention of the cabinetry craftsman, Gabe Feiurstein, who met his exacting specifications. He also credits two Manhattan antique shops, Ann Morris and Vito Giallo, with providing many of his finds. **E.C.**

On Hollywood Boulevard

The Los Angeles apartment of Robert Mentzer
dramatizes a spectacular view

When Robert D. Mentzer, ASID, decided to set up his design practice in Los Angeles approximately ten years ago, his first apartment had what he called "a New York rather than a typical California look," meaning one with dark backgrounds and a rather formal, sophisticated design plan. (See *Interior Design,* July 1975). Since then, his address has changed several times, and with each new one he has made a different design statement.

The most recent is in a condominium building overlooking Hollywood Boulevard. The view, or more accurately, the views, are breathtaking. To the south there is downtown Los Angeles, Century City and—on clear days—Santa Monica and the Palos Verdes Peninsula. From the terrace, there are the Hollywood Hills with the famous "Hollywood" sign perched on the hillside. The entire plan of the apartment is devised not only to take advantage of these panoramic vistas but to enhance and dramatize them.

Classified as a one-bedroom apartment, the original layout had a large L-shaped living area. The "L" has been walled off to create a study/den that also serves as a guest room, and the living area side of the wall is mirrored to reflect the view. The end wall of the dining area is also mirrored so that no matter where one sits, the view can be seen either directly or reflected.

Colors and materials are purposely low key—white walls, charcoal gray contract grade carpet; black and white upholstery fabrics. Vertical blinds are used at all the windows, and the vast expanse of glass has been broken by the addition of reveals against which the blinds fold when they are drawn back.

The overall environment has a controlled casualness which is both inviting and relaxing, the kind of environment which, in the words of the designer, "makes people feel free to lounge and put their feet up."   **S.R.E.**

Opposite page and overleaf: Night and daytime views of the living room. By night, the city becomes a mural of twinkling lights; by day, an architectural landscape. Window reveals were added to serve as pockets for the vertical blinds when drawn (they are closed only in late afternoon to shield the rays of the sun). Seating pieces, in white channel-quilted upholstery, were designed for lounging; the Louis XVI open armchair and pillows are covered in black satin used for men's tuxedo lapels; accessories on the Italian marble-top table include an antique African mask, English Sheffield silver candlesticks, and a black lacquered box with ivory inlay.

Photographer: Toshi Yoshimi

On Hollywood Boulevard

Above and opposite page: Study/guest room was created by adding a divider wall closing off the "L" portion of the living room; the sofa converts to a bed; built-in bookshelves flank an antique French buffet; the painting above it is of 17th century Flemish origin and is not on canvas but wood panels.

Left: In the master bedroom, mirror—the same height as the windows—wraps around the bed and the adjoining wall; the opposite wall has illuminated niches housing books, accessories and television; colored sheets are used in place of a conventional bedspread.

The Mellowing of a Designer

*William Gaylord's San Francisco flat is evolving
as his concepts of décor and ambience are enlarged*

Several years ago when William Gaylord completed the design of his San Francisco flat in an 1870 Russian Hill building it was all elegantly engineered spareness—travertine flooring, custom carpeting, padded silk and suede walls, polished chrome cantilevered hearth and mantel. And scarcely an extraneous object in sight. Even the dogs—a matched pair of svelte gray whippets—seemed coordinated with the bare-bones, no-color sophistication of the place.

Today the whippets have been joined by a spirited Persian kitten who finds padded silk walls ideal for climbing, and the austerely placed art and neutral functional objects now nestle with exuberant flowering plants and timeless Orientalia.

A red lacquer and gilt Chinese tray chest reflects itself before the chromed fireplace. Rich cerulean and gilt 18th-Century Chinese storage pots glow on a Chippendale console. Giant succulents flourish where once a pair of retiring bottle trees stood. The beautiful basics of Billy Gaylord's flat have been enriched and enlivened. Acquisition no longer equates with clutter to this mellowing designer.

"I've learned how I want to live," is how Billy Gaylord explains this transformation. "I want to introduce intimacy and warmth. I don't want to intimidate. I want people who visit here to remember it with a warm glow."

The flat was originally planned for entertaining eight —an assumption by the designer of how he thought he would live and entertain in this, his first full scale apartment. The 28' by 28' living room that he created was designed with two separate seating groups for five and eight, and the dining table was scaled to seat eight. "But I found I almost never use the dining table," says Mr Gaylord. "I always seem to have either four for dinner, and we use a folding table before the fireplace, or I have 24 and everyone sits wherever."

So, formal arrangements have given way to more relaxed civilities as a maturing designer learns new ways to delight the eye and, indeed, evolves his personal design for living. Billy Gaylord is now at the place in his development as a designer where he can trust his own spontaneity. **L.W.G.**

Photographer: Jaime Ardiles-Arce

Enrichment of an austerely beautiful décor has evolved in Billy Gaylord's flat.

Above: The uninhibited assemblage on the *faux ivoire* top of a George I bedroom table is a case in point for Mr. Gaylord's new attitude toward acquisition and display. The head is a 26th Dynasty Egyptian death mask.

Opposite: Red lacquer and gilt Chinese tray table faces the chrome hearth in the living room. Lightweight bamboo table is one of several in the room meant for ready repositioning as seating is moved to accommodate varying numbers of guests. Beyond, the travertine dining table is poised on a chrome pedestal before an entry framed in chromed elements. The celadon urn is another recent addition to a mellowing décor.

Wall of windows with a deck beyond is supplemented with a large skylight in the living room of William Gaylord's transformation of a flat in an 1870 shingled house on San Francisco's Russian Hill. A sophisticated lighting system throughout involves 94 recessed ceiling and floor lights controlled both by a master switch and with a separate concealed control panels in each room. Pale leather seating, tables of travertine wedges separated by polished steel dowels, and the carpeting patterned in stylized Gs are among the elements designed by Mr. Gaylord. A pair of Louis XVI chairs are matched by a pair of uncanny reproductions. The seemingly formidable cacti are actually Euphorbia, low-maintenance, smooth-skinned succulents. Massive cerulean and gilt storage jars are poised on a Chippendale console before a Ron Davis painting. Egyptian Sarcophagus, circa 500-400 B.C., is suspended by polished steel dowels over a travertine plinth, echoing the design of the tables.

The Mellowing of a Designer

Suede-lined bedroom—even to the shutters detailed with chrome automobile trim—is a warmly enclosed setting utilizing the custom carpeting introduced in the living room. **Above:** Mr. Gaylord designed the small fireplace with raised hearth and the marble and mirror bathroom beyond.

Opposite: Another element of an enrichment process includes the recent introduction of custom wool braid to the camel hair bed curtains. The channel-tufted leather bed is topped with a lynx throw. Bedroom shelves, like those in the living room, slide into place like drawers. George I gilt table, also seen above, has a *faux ivoire* top.

The Mellowing of a Designer

Photographer: Jaime Ardiles-Arce

In apartment living, the concepts of luxurious living and large spaces are not necessarily mutually exclusive. Take, for example, designer William Whiteside's San Francisco flat—essentially just two rooms with a total area of about 700 square feet. Yet, as the photographs show, no compromise has been made in creating a setting of constrained opulence. A play of textures and materials, the large scale of the custom seating pieces, and the designer's personal collection of art, antiques and accessories are the primary elements used to achieve the desired effect.

The apartment, Whiteside explains, was originally part of a 20-room mansion designed by Willis Polk, circa 1904. Years ago, the dwelling was converted into four residential units; that which Whiteside occupies was originally the main drawing room and library—both heavy with redwood mouldings.

The living room is just 17' x 22', yet Whiteside has created an undeniable aura of luxury by using such elements as raw silk upholstery fabrics, *faux bois* finished woodworking, a brass and crackle lacquer custom drum table, and unusual accessories collected during travels. The sleeping niche, fitted with a bed, has walls finished with the same raw silk and travertine shelves. The painting is by Hassel Smith; the bronze sculpture is by Pomodoro.

Small on Space, Big on Luxury

The 700-square-foot San Francisco flat of designer William Whiteside

This page: The dressing room has storage compartments concealed behind the draped linen fabric.

Opposite: Brass panels and inlays in the coffered redwood ceiling have been added to bring light and sparkle into the windowless dining room. On a more pragmatic note, the brass panels conceal library shelving and storage for bar and table ware, as well as close off the area from the galley kitchen.

Because this is a rental facility, Whiteside sought to limit the amount of permanent improvements. He made no structural alterations, but as starting point did have all the architectural woodwork bleached and given a *faux bois* finish to harmonize with the neutral monochromatic setting he was to create. "I wanted to visually enlarge the space, and did so by keeping the background simple," he says. Thus, walls are a lightly glazed off-white shade, formerly heavy beams have been painted out, the floor covering throughout is sisal, and all upholstery fabrics are the same raw silk.

Of spatial constrictions, the designer says: "It's like living in a ship; everything has to have its place." He then goes on to describe some of his clever storage solutions. The pedestals for plants and objects are specially designed hollow containers that conceal stereo speakers. All other stereo equipment and video apparatus have been built into a closet near the sleeping niche, with the television on a moveable cart. Since clothing closets were short of adequate, Whiteside had his dressing area fitted with storage compartments concealed behind draped linen fabric. In the dining room, he had brass panels constructed to conceal storage space for bar and tableware and for library shelving. Also, a panel closes off the dining room from the adjacent galley kitchen. Brass, which has also been integrated into the coffered redwood ceiling, was selected to bring a degree of light and sparkle into a windowless chamber.

Whiteside hesitates to claim an identifiable stamp. But, he does say that this project exemplifies some of his adhered-to tenets. His interiors, he says, are "rich, sumptuous and comfortable, but not pretentious." This space, he continues, "is designed to be lived in, not looked at. It's not intimidating."   **E.C.**

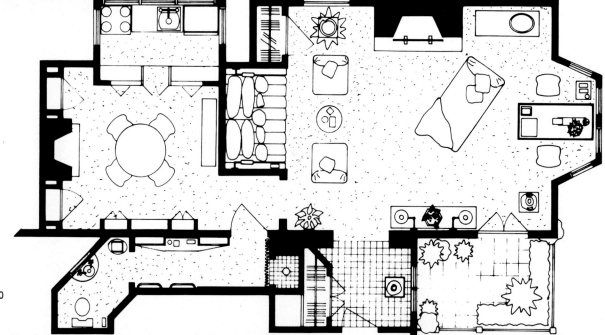

Photographers

Jaime-Ardiles-Arce
663 5th Ave.
New York, NY 10021
212/355-5022

Ivan Graae
Ivanovitsch
5 Dr. Tvaergade
DK-1302 Copenhagen
Denmark   01-114121

Elliot Fine
800 Carroll St.
Brooklyn, NY 11215
212/622-6613

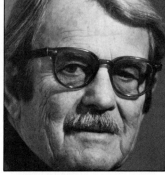

William Hedrich
Hedrich-Blessing
11 West Illinois St.
Chicago, IL 60610
312/321-1151

Dan Forer
1970 NE 149th St.
North Miami, FL 33181
305/949-3131

L. Blaine Hickey
Ogden Robertson
Hickey-Robertson
1318 Sul Ross
Houston, TX 77006
713/522-7258

Sheldon B. Lettich
5225 Wilshire Blvd. #1102
Los Angeles, CA 90036
213/933-2291 • 939-0023

Mark Ross
345 East 80th St.
New York, NY 10021
212/744-7258

Ogden Robertson

Norman McGrath
164 West 79th St.
New York, NY 10024
212/799-6422

Peter Vitale
157 East 71st St.
New York, NY 10021
212/249-8412

Ashod Kassabian
127 East 59th St.
New York, NY 10022
212/268-6480 • 421-1950

Peter Paige
37 West Homestead Ave.
Palisades Park, NJ 07650
201/592-7889

Toshi Yoshimi
4030 Camero Ave.
Los Angeles, CA 90027
213/660-9043

Interior Designers

Davis Allen
Skidmore, Owings and Merrill
220 East 42nd St.
New York, NY 10017
213/852-0867

Robert Bray

Illya Hendrix
Hendrix/Allardyce
550 N. Westbourne Dr.
Los Angeles, CA 90048
213/654-2222

Connie Beale
80 Mason St.
Greenwich, CT 06830
203/629-3442

Robert Bray
Michael Schaible
Bray-Schaible
80 West 40th St.
New York, NY 10018
212/354-7525

Thomas Allardyce

Raymond W. Boorstein
2020 NE 163rd St. Suite 108
North Miami Beach, FL 33162
305/940-0832

Michael Schaible

Marcel Bretos
41 East 42nd St.
New York, NY 10017
212/490-1185

Arthur Ferber
16 West 16th St.
New York, NY 10011
212/929-7757

Billy W. Francis
1707 West Gray
Houston, TX 77019
713/520-6100

Charles Gwathmey
Robert Siegel
Gwathmey-Siegel
475 10th Ave.
New York, NY 10018
212/947-1240

Angus John Bruce
A.J.B. and Co. Ltd.
398 West Broadway
New York, NY 10012
212/226-8658

Roger McKean Bazeley
245 East 63rd St.
Suite 1627
New York, NY 10021
212/888-0096

Tonny Foy
Boswell-Foy Associates
5300 Pershing St.
Fort Worth, TX 76107
817/732-1682

Robert Siegel

Michael de Santis
1110 Second Ave.
New York, NY 10022
212/753-8871

Richard Fitzgerald
7 Louisiana Square
Boston, MA 02108
617/742-1450

Billy Gaylord
1210 Lombard St.
San Francisco, CA 94109
415/947-1240

Noel Jeffrey
22 East 65th St.
New York, NY 10021
212/535-0300

Interior Designers

Steven Levine
Laverne Dagras

1133 Broadway
New York, NY 10010
212/243-3521

Robert Martin
1385 York Avenue
New York, NY 10021
212/535-2567
The Village Shops
Williamsburg, VA 23185
804/229-7500

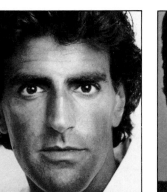

Mario Lo Cicero
343 West 71st St.
New York, NY 10023
212/873-2439

Robert Lewis
300 East 59th St.
New York, NY 10022
212/755-1557

Laverne Dagras

Vicente Wolf
Bob Patino
Patino-Wolf Assoc. Inc.
400 East 52nd St.
New York, NY 10022
212/355-6581

Anthony Machado
8251 Melrose Ave.
Los Angeles, CA 90046
213/852-0867

Robert Mentzer
9009 Beverly Blvd.
Los Angeles, CA 90048
213/276-2317 • 275-8310

Juan Montoya
80 Eighth Ave.
New York, NY 10010
212/852-0867

Bob Patino

Don Powell
Robert Kleinschmidt
Powell/Kleinschmidt
115 South La Salle St.
Suite 2208
Chicago, IL 60603
312/726-2208

Luis A. Rey
McMillen Inc.
155 East 56th St.
New York, NY 10022
212/753-5600

Sig Udstad
George Dandridge
Udstad-Dandridge Assoc.
59 East 54th St.
New York, NY 10022
212/755-3630

Ken Walker
Walker Group
304 East 52nd St.
New York, NY 10017
212/689-3013

Robert Kleinschmidt

Cloud Rich, Inc.
144 East 24th St.
New York, NY 10010
212/677-9500

George Dandridge

Kevin Walz
Walz Design
141 Fifth Ave.
New York, NY 10010
212/477-2211

Adam Tihany
130 East 61st St.
New York, NY 10021
212/355-6119

William Whiteside
84 Vanderwater St.
San Francisco, CA 94133
415/381-0193

Yung Wang
411 East 87th St.
New York, NY 10028
212/289-8531

Sources

Sources